CLOSE READING
OF INFORMATIONAL TEXTS

Close Reading of Informational Texts

ASSESSMENT-DRIVEN INSTRUCTION IN GRADES 3–8

Sunday Cummins

Foreword by Camille Blachowicz

THE GUILFORD PRESS
New York   London

Library of Congress Cataloging-in-Publication Data

Cummins, Sunday.
    Close reading of informational texts : assessment-driven instruction in grades
3–8 / by Sunday Cummins.
        pages cm
    Includes bibliographical references and index.
    ISBN 978-1-4625-0781-8 (pbk. : alk. paper)—ISBN 978-1-4625-0785-6
(cloth : alk. paper)
    1. Language arts (Elementary)   2. English language—Composition and
exercises—Study and teaching (Elementary)   3. Exposition (Rhetoric)—Study
and teaching (Elementary)   I. Title.
    LB1576.C854 2013
    372.6—dc23
                                                                    2012035267

About the Author

Sunday Cummins, PhD, is a literacy consultant and facilitator for the New Schools Project at the Erikson Institute in Chicago. Formerly, she was Assistant Professor of Education in the Reading and Language Department at National Louis University. Prior to teaching at National Louis, Dr. Cummins worked in the public schools for 10 years as a middle school and third-grade teacher and as a literacy coach. Dr. Cummins has written articles for *The Reading Teacher* and *Talking Points*, and shares her work on teaching with informational texts by presenting at state, national, and international conferences. Her website is *www.Sunday-Cummins.com*.

Foreword

The Common Core State Standards place a high priority on the close,
sustained reading of complex text, beginning with Reading Standard 1.
Such reading focuses on what lies within the four corners of the text.
                                    —COLEMAN AND PIMENTEL (2012, p. 4)

Overheard in the teachers' room as teachers study the standards:

Well, they mention "close reading" all the time. What is "close reading"?

I guess it's just reading carefully.

What's new about that?

They must mean something special—what are "the four corners of the text"?

Help!!!!!!!

Conversations such as this are likely to occur all over the United States as the Council of Chief State School Officers continues the development of the Common Core State Standards (CCSS) and encourages the formation of state assessments that match these standards. Yet the creators of these standards clearly state that implementation is in the hands of teachers:

> By emphasizing required achievements, the Standards leave room for teachers, curriculum developers, and states to determine how those goals should be reached and what additional topics should be addressed. Thus, the Standards do not mandate such things as a particular writing process or the full range of metacognitive strategies that students may need to monitor and direct their thinking and learning. Teachers are thus free to provide students with whatever tools and knowledge their professional judgment and experience identify as most helpful for meeting the goals set out in the Standards. (Common Core State Standards Initiative, 2010, p. 4)

Like the teachers just mentioned, I know that implementing new standards is a tall order! My concern for teachers, as they work to connect the best practices they know and use in classrooms to the CCSS, makes me very excited for the potential of this book as a key resource. Sunday Cummins is a well-regarded teacher-educator, who is knowledgeable about best practices and contemporary educational standards and who has extensive experience in classrooms as well. Her expertise shows on every page of this volume.

The term *close reading* emerged from the literary criticism of the 1920s to the 1970s and refers to the careful reading of sections of literary texts, paying particular attention to every aspect of their composition—how the sentences are put together, what vocabulary is used, and so forth. Cummins repurposes this term for educators of the 21st century by connecting it to the need to grapple with informational text and to read across a range of informational sources in order to engage in complex problem solving. The ultimate goal is for students to take a stance—to closely evaluate informational texts and, in the process, to develop the critical thinking skills they will need as readers, as students, and as citizens.

This is a challenging task for teachers, of course, and the careful construction of this book guides them through the instructional practices and strategies they need to implement close reading and other important comprehension goals in the classroom. Take a moment to think about what you are doing as you read this foreword. You are tapping your knowledge of text structure, vocabulary, and topic to understand what I am saying. You have a purpose for reading and probably some questions about close reading. You may want an overview of and introduction to the book, or perhaps you are deciding if you want to read further. You are constantly registering what you comprehend or stopping if you don't understand to rethink, review, or react. You are selecting what is most important about what is being said and then synthesizing this information into your conclusions and reactions. All these actions are essential for us as teachers and for the students we teach.

The first chapter of this book delineates the essential skills and strategies readers need to carry out close reading and presents the learning goals for students. Subsequent chapters provide a road map of an instructional approach that facilitates the journey. Dr. Cummins's model of assessment-directed instruction is not a simple test–retest model, but rather a thoughtful approach that includes all the necessary steps in the process—including student self-assessment, which is so often neglected. The author is honest and realistic in cautioning readers that this approach does not provide "quick answers" but instead requires "a commitment to a series of lessons over time that build on one another, . . . pushing for conceptual understanding of the strategies taught" (Coleman & Pimentel, 2012, p. 4). The good news is that having presented the goal and the road map for achieving it, she makes all the right stops along the way that a teacher needs to make to do an effective job.

What quickly emerges is what I call the author's "genius move"—starting with synthesis. Too often, in taxonomy-driven instruction, students never develop the skill of synthesizing because they never quite get through the other foundational comprehension strategies thought to be prerequisites. Cummins begins her instructional work with this important comprehension ability by using interactive read-alouds to give students the feel of the whole endeavor of close reading and comprehending. The teacher reads and thinks aloud, models the gathering and using of evidence, and lets students use this modeled comprehension as the basis for their accountable talk, discussion, and writing. This process is much like a parent running alongside a child who is learning to ride a new bike, holding the bike for balance to give the new rider the *feel* of riding before actually riding independently. It also allows all students to enjoy challenging literature, which is especially important for making informational content available to those whose reading or language skills are still developing.

The core of the book consists of example- and lesson-rich chapters on the strategies needed for effective close reading of informational text. Each and every example, activity, book selection, assessment, and teacher comment comes from real teachers working with real students in real classrooms. The authenticity shines through, and I'm sure you will recognize your work and that of your colleagues as you read through these lessons and visualize what they should look like. The thoughtful questions in the closing Study Guide can also assist you in using this book as a professional learning group resource for staff development or for mentoring new teachers and teachers-in-training.

Finally, this book is beautifully written and is really a great informational read! The examples not only will make you think, they will make you smile at the thoughtful creativity of the students and the teachers who have contributed to the book. This is a wonderful road map for teaching effective close reading of informational texts. The journey is as enjoyable as the destination is important. I learned from it as I enjoyed the ride, and you will too!

CAMILLE BLACHOWICZ, PhD
National College of Education
National Louis University

■ References

Coleman, D., & Pimentel, S. (2012). *Publishers' criteria for the Common Core State Standards in English language arts and literacy, grades 3–12*. Retrieved May 14, 2012, from *engageny.org/resource/criteria-for-common-core-aligned-elaliteracy-resources-grades-3-12*.

Common Core State Standards Initiative. (2010). *Common Core State Standards for English language arts and literacy in history/social studies, science, and technical subjects*. Washington, DC: National Governors Association Center for Best Practices and the Council of Chief State School Officers.

Acknowledgments

I want to extend a huge thank-you to the teachers and students who worked with me on the content of this book. These teachers opened their classroom doors wide, and hundreds of students shared their learning with me. A special thank-you as well to Amanda, Beth, and Lori for hosting my visits to these schools. I am grateful to my peers Deborah, Eileen, Liz, and Roberta, who spent time reading drafts of this book, giving me constructive feedback, and sharing their wisdom. I also wish to thank senior production editor Louise Farkas and everyone at The Guilford Press for their work on this book. A final thank-you to my family, especially my husband Stephen and my daughter Anna, who cheered me on through a very long process!

SUNDAY CUMMINS

Contents

Introduction

Why Teach "Close Reading" of Informational Texts?

During the past decade, the number of informational texts published for schools and the mass market has risen exponentially, making informational texts in the classroom considerably more accessible and useful for instruction than ever. Today's students encounter informational texts in a variety of media, including content-area textbooks, library books, magazines, and online texts. Increasingly, our intermediate- and middle-grade students are being asked to engage in *close reading* of complex texts. For example, the Common Core State Standards (CCSS) include achievement standards for reading informational texts that require being able to read closely and determine central ideas (Common Core State Standards Initiative, 2010). Similarly, the 21st-century skills advocated by Bellanca and Brandt (2010) would encourage and enable students to make useful connections between the ideas in multiple content-area texts in order to better engage in complex problem solving.

So, what is close reading of informational texts? Close reading, as described in this book, results when the reader analyzes any given text at the word or phrase level and also the paragraph and section levels. As the reader analyzes the text, he or she determines which details are most important and how these fit together logically to convey the author's central idea(s) or theme(s). As a result of close reading, the reader begins to critically evaluate these ideas or themes. These are essential skills for our students to cultivate in a world where they are constantly bombarded with information they need to understand in order to be active participants in society.

Despite much recent attention focused on close reading, there continues to be a pervasive problem. Many students continue to reveal they are not able to engage deeply with informational texts—determining what is important, summarizing and synthesizing the information (ACT, Inc., 2006). Some students get only "the gist" of the text, while others remember only the last detail they read. Conversely, some remember too much, wanting to recite every single detail they read. Many students are familiar with how to skim texts to locate answers to specific questions. But when you ask them to identify an author's central ideas and supporting evidence from a section of text or the whole text, or to tell you how they decided which details were important and which were not, they falter in their responses.

Does this sound familiar? What will happen when these students grow up to be adults that need to make mature, informed decisions in the complex global society in which they live? Being able to read informational texts closely—across all content areas—creates a path for being able to understand the world more deeply, for being able to engage in creation, innovation, critical thinking, and problem solving, as well as communication and collaboration—all essential skills in college and career success. For all these reasons, teaching close reading is an imperative.

There are loads of professional books on teaching with informational texts and/or teaching in the various content areas. These books cover a great deal of information that gives readers a quick peek at what instruction "looks like" when teaching a variety of lessons. This may well be appropriate, given your particular purpose in reading them. Several years ago, however, my response to these texts started becoming "Give me more . . . by giving me less"—*less* of the detailed discussion of the different genres, types of texts, and the multiple instructional strategies appropriate to each; and *more* about how to teach the strategies of determining what is important and how to synthesize ideas when reading informational texts. As part of *how* to teach, I also wanted to know how to assess what students were doing to make sense of texts and how to move them forward in their thinking.

As a classroom teacher, I started a long-term professional inquiry into how to teach close reading of informational texts to determine what is important and how to synthesize key ideas. When I left my own classroom, I continued to visit colleagues' classrooms to work and learn with the teachers and their students. The key questions that shaped my personal inquiry include: What happens after the first lesson? What do students reveal in their written responses and oral comments about their ability to read closely? How do we need to teach and assess them to continuously move them forward in their thinking and learning? This book represents my earnest attempt to document what my colleagues and I have learned during this pedagogical journey.

Teaching the close reading of informational texts is tricky, requiring a lot of perseverance on the part of both teachers and students. My goal is not to provide quick answers but rather to suggest ideas to contemplate as you reflect on your own instructional practices and techniques in this area of teaching. You know your own students, and you have had experiences in teaching with informational texts that you can draw upon as you read this book; as you probably realize, your background knowledge will significantly affect how you understand and use the ideas in this book. So, consider this reading experience as an ongoing dialogue with me as a colleague as we both undertake this inquiry. You can also visit my website at *www.Sunday-Cummins.com* to keep track of how I am continuing in this extended journey and to contribute to the knowledge base that a whole community of educators is co-creating there.

Here's another thought to consider as you begin to read this book. Recently I had the pleasure of working with a team of educators in developing a unit of study on the civil rights movement for a third-grade summer school program in an urban district. We used the principles elaborated in Wiggin and McTigue's (2005) *Understanding by Design* to engage in backward planning. The performance task devised for the end of the unit was for each student to write a persuasive essay about a civil rights leader and to participate in a pretended wax museum setting as that person. To summon up a vivid understanding of this time period and the key historical figures involved, we preselected text sets for each classroom that included trade books, Internet websites, particular poems, readers' theater scripts, and primary sources. (Examples of similar text sets for multiple grades are available at my website on a variety of subjects.) The guide for instruction we wrote incorporated numerous opportunities for students to interact with these sources, including lessons written specifically on teaching the "close reading" of informational texts. These particular lessons would be important when the students needed to engage in independent completion of their reading tasks.

I share this vignette because the instruction described in this book is at its best when integrated into a content-area unit of study. At some point within any unit of study, students have to independently engage in the close reading of informational texts to determine what is important and to synthesize the most relevant information. So, whether students are creating a timeline of the Civil War or a wiki site on global warming issues, they will have to know how to engage in using these skills at some point to complete the whole project. That's where the content of this book fits in: that is, it is not meant to describe a separate construct or series of lessons totally isolated from the larger purpose of instruction (although that is left for you to decide) but rather to support you and your students in effectively accessing information as you all endeavor to think critically, creatively, and collaboratively during a unit of study.

■ Overview of Chapters

Chapter 1 examines what it means to engage in a close reading of informational texts and describes what I believe to be the essential skills of close reading:

- Tapping one's prior knowledge of the text structure, vocabulary, and the specific topic.
- Setting one's purpose by previewing the text strategically.
- Self-monitoring for meaning.
- Determining importance.
- Synthesizing.

Chapter 2 sets forth an assessment-driven, structured approach to teaching that includes the following instructional components:

- Assessment of students' strengths and needs.
- Lesson preparation and text study.
- Focus lesson—explaining instructional objectives and modeling.
- Guided practice.
- Independent practice.
- Student self-assessment.

Central to making this instruction work is a commitment to a series of lessons over time that build on one another (through multiple content-area units of study), pushing for conceptual understanding of the strategies being taught, and continually assessing students' work in planning each lesson.

In Chapters 3–8, the core ideas underlying teaching and learning experiences with informational text are described. The chapters are aligned with the teaching continuum depicted in Figure I.1., with each chapter building on the skills taught in the preceding one. This process makes for a cohesive and coherent approach to instruction, thereby avoiding the fragmented instruction that might occur when

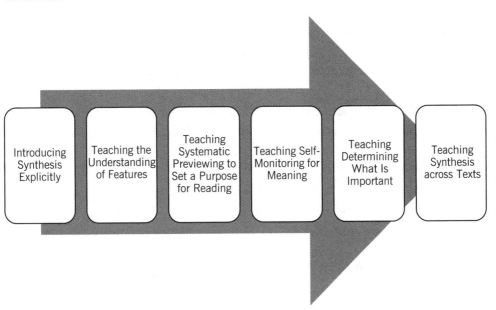

FIGURE I.1. Continuum of lessons for nurturing students' close reading of informational texts.

one strategy or another is taught here, there, and sometimes in between. The objective is to help students understand how they need to develop a set of well-honed skills to closely read and understand a text. While close reading specifically to determine which ideas are most important is taken up in detail in Chapter 7, all of the teaching and learning chapters include some element of close reading—that is, analyzing text at the word, sentence, and section levels. These chapters also include tools for assessing students' learning, samples of students' work, and descriptions of lessons designed to move students forward in their learning. (All students' names are pseudonyms.)

Chapter 3 describes how to explicitly introduce the strategy of synthesis by creating opportunities for students to listen to you reading aloud and thinking aloud. The lessons specifically include opportunities for the students to write in response to the texts that you read aloud. Teaching the students' how to employ textual evidence to support their synthesis of the text's key ideas is also explained.

Chapter 4 describes lessons on teaching how to closely read or examine the "features" that accompany informational text—such features as figures and captions, sidebars and boxes, and the like. This analysis includes considering how these various features support and extend the author's central ideas and then writing responses that reflect one's synthesis of what was learned.

Chapter 5 introduces the mnemonic "THIEVES" for previewing the text systematically in ways that help readers get one step ahead of the author and make relevant predictions and judgments about the author's central ideas.

Chapter 6 introduces an activity called "coding" that provides a concrete set of steps for continually monitoring for meaning while reading the running text. Students practice monitoring for new or unfamiliar information, for questions that may occur to them, and for instances where their natural, ongoing meaning making may suddenly break down.

Chapter 7 describes how to teach students how to go about determining what is important at the sentence, paragraph, and section levels while simultaneously synthesizing the whole text. Determining what is important is made easier when one can readily identify such text structures as description, sequence, comparison, cause–effect, and problem–solution, and these are addressed in this chapter as well.

Chapter 8 applies the learning gained in closely reading individual texts to the larger project of reading for information across multiple texts in order to write a short research report.

Finally, "Closing Thoughts" reviews the key ideas explored in this book and the Appendix presents a study guide that should help teachers implement the lessons described, chapter by chapter. Ideally, this Study Guide should be used in conjunction with other educators in a "professional learning community" that provides opportunities to look at students' work samples and have meaningful dialogues that deepen your mutual understanding of these teaching practices.

CHAPTER ONE

What Does "Close Reading" Mean?

Consider the following paragraph from the children's book *Frogs* (Bishop, 2008):

> Some frogs seek out their food. A toad hops around after dark, snapping up moths, beetles, and crickets. It may eat more than 5,000 insects during a single summer. Other frogs ambush their prey. A horned frog hides among leaves on the rain forest floor in South America. It stays absolutely still, day after day. When an animal comes by, the frog watches attentively, waiting until it moves closer. Then it seizes the prey with a loud snap of its huge mouth. The horned frog is not a fussy eater. It gulps down cockroaches, lizards, mice, and even other horned frogs. (p. 17)

A student reading for the gist of this paragraph might initially think, "This paragraph is about how frogs like the toad and horned frog seek out their food." But when the student stops to consider the details at the sentence and word levels, he or she soon realizes that the author has created a much richer picture supported by a variety of details.

Let's closely review the paragraph, sentence by sentence. The first sentence introduces the primary topic—how "frogs seek out their food." The second and third sentences describe how the toad finds its food and even state how many insects it can eat in just one summer—"5,000." The fourth sentence begins with the phrase *other frogs*, which signals to the reader that a contrast is about to be made. The fifth sentence introduces the "horned frog" and moves into a four-sentence descriptive sequence of the horned frog's ambush of its prey. This is followed by a sentence that describes the horned frog as "not a fussy eater." In the last sentence, there is an implied contrast. The reader can infer, based on the information shared in this sentence and the second sentence, that the toad and horned frog eat different creatures. Students reading to determine what is important by engaging in the act of close reading might say the following:

> Well, the author is describing how both the toad and the horned frog seek out their food. But he doesn't just give information about one and then the other. He describes these creatures' habits in such a way that I noticed the contrast between the two. They are very different in how they seek their food and in what they eat. I think this ties back to the theme in the book that frogs are highly diverse creatures.

In *Techniques for Close Reading*, Brummett (2010) defines close reading as "the mindful, disciplined reading of an object (i.e., text) with a view to deeper understanding of its meaning" (p. 3). When a student engages in "close reading," he or she analyzes the text at the word or phrase level and the sentence and paragraph levels. By considering the weight of meaning of particular phrases or sentences in a section of text, the student can begin to see how important details fit together to support the author's central idea in a section of the text or the whole text (in complex texts, there will be more than one central idea). Knowing how to go about engaging in this type of reading and making sure the reader fully attends to the act of reading are both essential. When a student is finished reading closely, he or she can identify the author's central ideas and describe why any particular idea is significant. He or she can also find supporting details in the text and explain how these serve as evidence substantiating the central ideas. This creates a basis for critiquing the author's ideas, thereby moving into deeper thinking about the text as a whole. The development of these skills is essential not only to students' ultimate academic success but also to their long-term ability to comprehend new information and use it for effective decision making as adults.

■ Meeting the Standards for Close Reading

In the Common Core State Standards (CCSS, 2010), the first two anchor standards for College and Career Readiness state that students who are college and career ready should be able to do the following with a grade-level text:

- Read closely to determine what the text says explicitly and to make logical inferences from it; cite specific textual evidence when writing or speaking to support conclusions drawn from the text.
- Determine central ideas or themes of a text and analyze their development; summarize the key supporting details and ideas.

The CCSS also include Reading Standards for Informational Text K–5 and 6–12, which are related to the two anchor standards listed above and that represent improved capabilities over time. Table 1.1 lists the basic standards for grades 3, 5, and 8. While the CCSS for grades 4, 6, and 7 are not included here, you can see how the expectations for student achievement in the area of higher-level thinking about the author's central ideas increase over time.

Similar expectations for achievement with informational texts are included in the CCSS Reading Standards for Literacy in History/Social Studies, Science, and Technical Subjects in grades 6–12. In addition, the importance of thinking carefully about key ideas and details is woven into the writing, speaking, and listening standards as well. For example, by the end of the fourth grade a student writing an informative text should be able to "develop the topic with facts, definitions, concrete details, quotations or other information and examples related to the topic" (p. 20). By the end of the sixth grade, a student giving an oral presentation should be able to "present claims and findings, sequencing ideas logically and using pertinent descriptions, facts, and details to accentuate main ideas or themes" (p. 49). To meet these standards and others, a student must *know how* to engage in close reading of a text.

TABLE 1.1. Reading Standards Related to Informational Text and Anchor Standards for Key Ideas and Details

Grade 3 students	Grade 5 students	Grade 8 students
Ask and answer questions to demonstrate understanding of a text, referring explicitly to the text as the basis for the answers.	Quote accurately from a text when explaining what the text says explicitly and when drawing inferences from the text.	Cite the textual evidence that most strongly supports an analysis of what the text says explicitly as well as inferences drawn from the text.
Determine the main idea of a text; recount the key details and explain how they support the main idea.	Determine two or more main ideas of a text and explain how they are supported by key details; summarize the text.	Determine a central idea of a text and analyze its development over the course of the text, including its relationship to supporting ideas; provide an objective summary of the text.

Note. Excerpted from Common Core State Standards (2010).

■ What Are the Essentials of Close Reading?

In order to read closely, a student must have a strong grasp of how informational texts are built as well as what close reading for deep understanding, or synthesis, of a text involves. The essential skills for close reading are described in Table 1.2 and include:

- Tapping one's prior knowledge related to informational text structure.
- Topical and vocabulary knowledge.
- Setting a purpose for reading.
- Self-monitoring for meaning.
- Determining what is important.
- Synthesizing.

Teaching these comprehension skills may feel familiar. These skills, or strategies, can be taught for a variety of purposes, however, including reading for enjoyment,

TABLE 1.2. The Repertoire of Skills Needed for Close Reading

Essential skills for close reading	Description
Tapping prior knowledge related to text structure	The reader uses knowledge about the structure of informational texts *and* strategies when tackling an unfamiliar text. This knowledge helps the reader begin to make predictions about the author's central ideas and create a strategic plan for how to go about reading the text.
Tapping prior topical and vocabulary knowledge	The reader activates and contrasts prior content-area knowledge with the content of the text being read. The reader also uses knowledge of content-related vocabulary to comprehend content in a text and effectively figure out the meaning of unfamiliar vocabulary in a text.
Setting a purpose	As the reader systematically previews the text, he or she begins to identify a clear reason for reading the text related to understanding the author's central ideas; the reader thereafter adjusts the purpose for reading as needed.
Self-monitoring for meaning	The reader identifies when meaning breaks down and flexibly and adaptively uses various approaches to repair meaning.
Determining what is important	The reader identifies specific information (details in the text at the word, phrase, paragraph, and section levels) that supports and extends the author's central idea.
Synthesizing	The reader identifies a central idea (theme) that emerges while reading the text and considers how the important details in that text fit together to convey that central idea. The reader reflects on how the knowledge conveyed in the central idea resonates with his or her prior knowledge and articulates how his or her thinking evolved while reading.

reading to answer a specific question, or reading to learn about a topic of interest. In this book the focus is on teaching students how to tap these strategies flexibly while they engage in closely reading informational text in order to identify the author's central ideas and supporting details.

For the purposes of this book, *reading skills* are defined as "automatic actions that result in decoding and comprehension with speed, efficiency, and fluency and usually occur without awareness of the components or control involved" (Afflerbach, Pearson, & Paris, 2008, p. 368). So, the term *reading skill* refers to what a reader does automatically without thinking, whereas *reading strategies* are about the reader being purposefully aware of his or her efforts to read and understand a text. In other words, when a student is "trying out" an approach to reading (perhaps during guided instruction with the teacher present to coach), the approach the student is using is a "reading strategy," but when the student's use of this approach becomes automatic, then this is a "reading skill."

While it is essential to reading informational texts closely, developing content-related vocabulary and topical background knowledge is not a direct focus of this text. However, if the lessons described in this book are implemented with content-area texts as part of a unit of study, the reading and writing the students engage in as part of the lessons do contribute toward developing their vocabulary and content-area knowledge.

Prior Knowledge of Text Structure

Prior knowledge has been defined as the knowledge students have developed as part of classroom learning (Fisher & Frey, 2009), whereas *background knowledge* is the knowledge students have developed from their own personal experiences. Regardless of when or where the knowledge was developed, there are two types of knowledge students need to activate to read informational texts successfully: knowledge related to the subject or topic of the text being read and structural knowledge related to the organization and features of informational texts.

If the student has topical knowledge related to the content in the text *and* knows how to tap that knowledge to help him or her understand the information in a new text, comprehension is more likely. This makes the case for engaging students in the lessons described in this book as part of instruction in a particular content-area unit of study. When we present students with informational texts on miscellaneous topics to teach specific reading strategies, we are handicapping what the students might be able to do if they were able to access the knowledge being built during content-area instruction. If, instead, we use informational texts related to the content-area unit *during* the literacy block, students will be able to activate knowledge they are currently immersed in developing and using at another point during the day.

That said, being able to tap students' knowledge of *how texts are structured* is just as important to reading for understanding. By "knowledge of how texts are structured," I mean knowledge of how an informational text will most likely be built. When we read an informational text and tap our prior knowledge of text structure, we realize that the author can employ several different "features"—illustrations and captions, side bars and boxed items, charts and figures, for example. In the prose of the text, there is probably an introduction that grabs your attention and a closing that encapsulates the author's central ideas. In the body of the text, the author probably organizes ideas into sections and uses section headings to give the reader an idea of the content that is addressed in that section. At the sentence, paragraph, section, and feature levels, the author may employ a variety of microstructures (i.e., compare and contrast, sequence, description, etc.) that help the reader make sense of the text.

This way of viewing "text structure" is different from the structures typically mentioned in the literature such as description/definition/example, sequence/time order, comparison, cause–effect, problem–solution, and so on. While the teaching of these specific structures is addressed in Chapter 7, my main approach in this book is to teach students to recognize these structures as just one part of what authors do to build texts. Given the variety and complexity of the informational texts available today, the chances are slim that authors will employ just one text structure. An author may use one text structure for a large portion of the text or just a section of the text. Often an author uses *multiple* structures even within a single section of text to develop a central idea. Let's consider the two-page spread on the digestive system shown in Figure 1.1, excerpted from a text on the human body (Stephens, 2002).

If you read the prose (the main body of the text) closely, you will notice that the author begins with an introduction that *describes* a daily scenario: you eat, and while you go on with your life your digestion system is hard at work. The second and third paragraphs serve to identify the *sequence* of digestion from the mouth, to the stomach, to the large intestine and beyond. If you read closely, however, the author is not only identifying the sequence of events but also describing the parts of the digestive system along the way. Consider the following sentences: "Lining the small intestine are millions of fingerlike structures called villi. Villi capture nutrients that are eventually carried away to feed the cells in your body." The first sentence describes the villi, and the second sentence identifies a step in

Digestive System

Salivary glands
Mouth
Esophagus
Stomach
Liver
Pancreas
Small intestine
Large intestine

Q When I think about food, my mouth waters. Why?

A Your brain is "telling" your salivary glands to make extra saliva. In your lifetime, you'll make enough saliva to fill about 200 bathtubs.

Q My stomach makes a lot of noise. What's all the rumbling?

A Before and after you eat, gases can be produced. These gases make noise as they gurgle along.

Q Why do I burp?

A Gases from digesting, as well as the air that you swallow while you eat, can build up in your stomach. When there's no room left, some of the gas can come back up in the form of a burp.

Where Does It Go?

You're sitting at lunch, finishing that last bit of sandwich and chomping on your apple. Then you head outside to play. In a few minutes, you're probably talking with friends and not thinking about the food you just ate. While you've moved on to other things, your body's **digestive system** is hard at work.

Digestion starts in the mouth, where your teeth cut and grind food into small pieces. Saliva, made by the salivary glands, wets and softens food. When you swallow, the food squeezes down a long tube, called the **esophagus**, into your stomach. The **stomach** churns your food and adds a digestive juice that turns the food into a soupy liquid. Muscles move the liquid into the small intestine.

In the **small intestine**, more digestive juices break food into tiny particles called nutrients. These digestive juices are made by organs, such as the **liver** and **pancreas**, and delivered to the small intestine. Lining the small intestine are millions of fingerlike structures called **villi**. Villi capture nutrients that are eventually carried away to feed the cells in your body. Any undigested food moves on to the **large intestine** where water is absorbed. The remaining material leaves the body as waste.

FIGURE 1.1. Two-page spread excerpted from *The Human Machine* (Stephens, 2002). Text reprinted by permission of Hampton-Brown and National Geographic Learning, a part of Cengage Learning. Copyright by National Geographic Learning. Reprinted by permission. All rights reserved. Images: Boy eating a snack reprinted by permission of Getty images; boy drinking at fountain and girl eating lunch reprinted by permission of Corbis images.

the sequence of the digestive process. Students need to understand the different types of details the author is including and then use that understanding to comprehend the key information. In other words, students need to be able to think: "Well, the author is mostly identifying the sequences involved in digestion, but at the same time she's describing the physical characteristics of some of the organs involved. For example, the esophagus is long, and the villi look like fingers."

The perception that students need to appreciate how authors routinely employ more than just one text structure is further confirmed when you consider the graphics on the two-page spread. To the left of the central text is a sidebar titled "I.Q.: Interesting Questions"; while the text in the sidebar appears to be in a question–answer format, the content of the questions and answers is in a reverse cause–effect text structure. For example, if you read the first question-and-answer combination, you learn that thinking about food (cause) makes you salivate (effect).

Turning our attention to the full page of graphic features on the second page of the spread, the three photographs of children eating serve to support the prose described earlier and the first step in the sequence—"digestion starts in the mouth." The graphic labeled "Digestive System," while not ideally suited to support an understanding of the sequence of digestion (because there are no features that indicate the precise pathway of the food moving from one organ to the next), does offer a fairly graphic visual representation of the organs involved in the process of digestion. If you decided to teach sequence text structure with this two-page spread of text in order for students to understand the exact sequencing of the digestive process, the students would also need to practice flexibility and know when the author is tapping a different text structure (in the graphics and at the sentence level).

The issue of identifying a particular text structure becomes even more problematic when you consider a more complex text, such as the following excerpt from an eighth-grade world history book (Spielvogel, 2005) that comprises the first section of a chapter on early humans. The author begins the chapter by describing how archaeologists and anthropologists study past societies and, as a result of their work, can tell us much about prehistoric peoples. The following excerpt starts with the section heading "Dating Artifacts and Fossils."

> One of the most important and difficult jobs of both archaeologists and anthropologists is dating their finds. Determining the age of human fossils makes it possible to understand when and where the first humans emerged. Likewise, the dating of artifacts left by humans helps scientists understand the growth of early societies.

How, then, do archaeologists and anthropologists determine the ages of the artifacts and fossils they find? One valuable method is radiocarbon dating. All living things absorb a small amount of radioactive carbon (C-14) from the atmosphere. After a living thing dies, it slowly loses C-14. Using radiocarbon dating, a scientist can calculate the age of an object by measuring the amount of C-14 left in it.

Radiocarbon dating, however, is only accurate for dating objects that are no more than about 50,000 years old. Another method—thermoluminescence dating—enables scientists to make relatively precise measurements back to 200,000 years. This method of analysis dates an object by measuring the light given off by electrons trapped in the soil surrounding the fossils and artifacts. (p. 20)

Within just three paragraphs of this voluminous textbook, the author has used multiple structures at the micro level (i.e., the sentence and paragraph levels), and no clear macrostructure is revealed. To really understand this text, to read this text closely, a student has to think not only about the content (this is where domain-specific vocabulary and topical background knowledge may prove helpful) but also how the author is structuring the language to convey the content—at the word, sentence, and paragraph levels.

In the first sentence of the excerpt, the author identifies the central idea. This is also a claim, because he identifies the job of "dating their finds" as "important and difficult." He gives reasons (or warrants) for this claim in the form of two sentences with *cause–effect* structures. In the first sentence of the second paragraph, the author identifies the topic of the following text in the form of a question (i.e., *problem*) and then goes on to give an *example* of one method of dating artifacts (i.e., *solution*). He does not continue, as one might expect, by describing the method but instead engages in a complex structure that reveals the *cause–effect* relationship between living things, dead things, and the amount of radioactive carbon absorbed or lost. Finally, one effect of these relationships is that scientists are able to calculate the age of the dead thing, as implied in the paragraph's final sentence. In the first two sentences of the third paragraph, the author *compares* one method of carbon dating with another, and he then proceeds to *describe* the second method in the last sentence. Ideally, a close reading of this text would enable the reader to consider the microstructures the author employs. That is, the student would be able to name, describe, and contrast the two methods of artifact dating and draw conclusions about why these methods are important to archaeologists and anthropologists.

The point is this: teaching students the traditionally identified text structures has only limited value unless we also help them to understand how these structures are used *flexibly* by most authors to convey certain points. While a text may be written perfectly for teaching a particular structure like compare and contrast, often the next text the student reads on the same content-area topic is *not* structured that way. Pointing out a few instances of a text with a particular structure will not necessarily help students in the long run. What they need instead, is to develop a larger understanding of how texts are structured and then engage in repeated exercises applying this knowledge to new texts.

So, what we know about how an informational text is structured or built is part of our schema, or prior knowledge. We need to tap this knowledge when we read informational texts, and we need to avoid considering our schema as merely isolated bits of knowledge that we tap only occasionally. We need to consider our schema as organized into categories, such as one labeled "this is what I know about how informational texts are structured" and another "this is what I know about how to use that knowledge to tackle new informational texts." This way of understanding schema represents a conceptual approach to teaching for *understanding informational text structure as a whole*. So, while we may instruct students about the particular features of informational text or the included details that convey cause–effect relationships, these smaller instructional moments are part of a larger long-term conversation with our students about the multiple ways in which authors structure or build their texts to convey their central ideas. Chapter 4 addresses how to teach students to understand the features accompanying informational text, and Chapter 7 offers some ideas for teaching at the macro- and microtext structure level.

What Should Setting a Purpose for Reading Look Like?

Outside of school, we never read without a purpose or a reason. We may read a newspaper to learn more about current political events or to find out what is happening locally over the weekend. We may read emails from friends for enjoyment or emails from our child's teacher for important information we need to know. Our purposes vary depending on the type of text we are reading and our interests or needs. Purposes are central to any reading we do, and therefore the concept of "the purpose for reading" needs to be considered carefully whenever we think about how to teach the close reading of informational texts.

The various purposes for reading informational texts have long been listed in professional books and are even readily available on made-for-classroom wall posters. These purposes include mainly the following: to be informed, to follow directions, to be entertained, and to learn how to do something. While there is some value in explicitly sharing these purposes with students, we have to be careful that they don't then begin to use these lists to just mindlessly "fill in the blank" in expressing their purpose for reading. During one lesson, for example, I asked a fifth-grade student about his purpose for reading an assigned article on the dramatic impact of a volcano's explosion on the surrounding community. Instantly he replied, "I am reading for information on volcanoes." There appeared to be no depth of understanding or "ownership," behind his answer; rather, he seemed to be simply regurgitating what he had been taught.

The challenge is to broaden students' understanding of "purpose." A meaningful purpose gives the reader a deep resolve to get at what the author is trying to say, to get at the *author's purpose* in writing the text. A reader's purpose has to be more than simply "I'm reading to find out more about volcanoes." One way to instill greater purpose in readers is to teach them how to *preview* the text and make relevant predictions. The students can use these predictions to set clearer and more meaningful purposes for their reading. Under this scenario, a student's purpose for reading the article on the volcano eruption might be expressed more likely in this way:

> I want to find out why on earth this author would want to write about the eruption of this particular volcano. When I previewed the text, I started thinking he is writing about this one volcano's eruption, and, based on the pictures, it looks like the eruption had a huge impact on the animals and homes and people who lived nearby. Why does the author think this is so important for me to know—so important that I should spend time reading his text?

Embedded within a set purpose there also has to be a little bit of what our students might call "attitude." In a way, you are challenging the author to a conversation of sorts. It's almost as if mentally the student has to say something like the following:

> You, the author, better make your central ideas clear to me, and you can't just say what you think. You need to back your ideas up with evidence—strong evidence and details that make clear what you are trying to say. I want to walk away from you and your text with some new ideas to ponder. And even that isn't enough! As the reader, I'm still going to be critiquing how you put all of this together and evaluating your ideas. So, be ready!

Of course, your initial purpose for reading can shift and deepen as you read further. Some students make erroneous predictions early on and, as a result, set purposes for their reading that lead them astray from what the text is communicating. For example, when I read an article titled "Thirsty Planet" (Geiger, 2010) with a group of fifth graders, the article's first two pages included the title and a close-up picture of villagers from Marsbit, Kenya, filling jugs with water from a well. One student wrote as her prediction, "Pollution is overruling the planet so bad [that] people can't even drink clean water." Actually, there is no mention of pollution at all in this article, the article focusing instead on how water is a finite resource and we have to be careful about how we use it. The student had assumed (without any textual evidence to support the assumption) that the water in the well was dirty. This served to influence her prediction and, as a result, the purpose she set for reading. To help this student, we need to teach her how to make better predictions (based on evidence previewed in the text) and, as a backup plan, to adjust her predictions and the purposes she sets for reading as she continues to read.

Readers may also need to adjust their purposes for reading from one section of text to another or even from one paragraph to the next. In the article "Thirsty Planet" (Geiger, 2010), the author describes how plants use water, then how animals use water, and then how humans use water. The reader may pick up the central idea that water is used by every living thing for survival in some way; as the reader moves from one section of the text to another, his or her purpose might be "I'm reading to find out what yet another living thing does with water." Then, toward the end of the article, the author shifts, writing "With so many demands on our fresh water supply, do we have enough?" and includes a description of how fresh water is not evenly distributed throughout the world. The reader at that point has to shift with the author in assessing his or her purpose for reading. In a sense, the reader has to say:

> I was reading to find out more about how living things use water, and I learned a lot about the importance of water to living things. Now I need to read and think about how access to fresh water might be a problem that needs solving.

The point is that students will likely fail at reading closely if they just start to read a text with no purpose in mind. They must set a purpose meaningful enough for them to spend the energy required for close reading. One way to start teaching this approach is to demonstrate to students how to preview the text systematically and make relevant predictions about the author's purpose in writing the text. Students feel empowered when they know more about what the text will be about and, as a result, can more easily set a helpful purpose for their own reading. Chapter 5 addresses teaching students how to go about effectively setting a purpose for reading by using the mnemonic THIEVES and how to assess students' previewing and prediction skills.

What Does Self-Monitoring for Meaning Look Like?

Self-monitoring is about knowing when we understand the content we are reading (at the word, sentence, and section or whole-text levels) and knowing what to do when our meaning making breaks down. Take a moment to reread the extract from the eighth-grade world history textbook (Spielvogel, 2005) on pages 14–15. As you read, consider the following:

- What are you reading that you already know?
- What are you reading that is less familiar? What did you do to better help you to understand this part? Slow down? Reread? Try to make connections to prior knowledge?
- What are your questions about what you are reading? Do your questions involve not understanding particular vocabulary words?

Now, let me demonstrate how I self-monitored when I read the third paragraph in the excerpt. (Please remember that I am not a scientist and I am not a history teacher, so I am very much the layperson when it comes to reading a text like this!) When I approached this third paragraph, I had set the purpose of reading to find out more about how archaeologists and anthropologists date the fossils and artifacts they find. Here, again, is the excerpted third paragraph:

> Radiocarbon dating, however, is only accurate for dating objects that are no more than about 50,000 years old. Another method—thermoluminescence dating—enables scientists to make relatively precise measurements back to 200,000 years. This method of analysis dates an object by measuring the light given off by electrons trapped in the soil surrounding the fossils and artifacts. (p. 20)

In the first sentence, when I read the word *however*, I thought, "Uh-oh. The word *however* means the author is probably going to introduce a new idea that contrasts in some way with the method of radiocarbon dating that I just read about in the second paragraph." What was I doing to self-monitor? Analyzing the text structure at the word and sentence levels.

Then I read on and got stuck on the word *thermoluminescence*, which I then reread a couple of times just to get the rhythm of reading the word fluently. I thought:

> What does this mean? I know *luminescent* has something to do with light and the
> prefix *thermo* means heat. So, does this method have something to do with light and
> heat? The author will probably define or describe this method, so I'm going to keep
> reading.

What was I doing to self-monitor? Analyzing the text at the word level; breaking the word into meaningful chunks; predicting that I would be able to make
or create more meaning, based on my understanding of how authors go about
developing their ideas.

I continued reading the rest of the second sentence and noticed that the
author introduced another amount of time—200,000 years. This made me think
"Wait, he stated an amount of time in the first sentence. I'm going to reread." I
reread the first sentence and thought:

> Yes! Radiocarbon dating can date artifacts back to 50,000 years, but this other
> method can get closer to 200,000 years. I'm saying "closer" instead of "exactly"
> because the author uses the words *relatively precise*. Well, that's an odd pair of
> words. Okay, so one method can date objects further back—by a lot more years—
> than the other. I get the contrast now, but I still don't understand what *thermolumi-
> nescence* is. I'm going to keep reading.

What was I doing to self-monitor? Analyzing the text at the sentence level, determining what was important (the specific number of years), and using that information to get a better understanding of the author's meaning.

Then I read the last sentence: "This method of analysis dates an object by
measuring the light given off by electrons trapped in the soil surrounding the fossils and artifacts." I was totally baffled and thought, "Well, I knew this method
had something to do with 'light,' and now the author has described how this
method dates an object, but I'm not really sure exactly what this means or looks
like." I reread the sentence a couple of times and checked out the features on the
page. "Not much help," I decided, and then I thought to myself:

> Well, my purpose was to know that dating artifacts and fossils is important and dif-
> ficult and also to learn more about how scientists date artifacts. The author makes a
> short case of why this is important, and this was nothing I didn't already know. I can
> surmise that these methods are difficult because I can't completely understand what
> they are, but I'm not sure the author really made a case for how difficult this is. If I
> was a scientist, I'd know what I was doing. Maybe the author was just trying to say
> that it's not easy to figure out how old the oldest artifacts are because we can only

go back so far in time with the dating. Finally, I can at least name two methods and sort of describe what they have to do with—radiocarbon dating, which has to do with how much carbon is in a fossil, and thermoluminescence, which has something to do with the light from electrons.

What did I do? I realized that my meaning making was breaking down and tried to repair the situation by thinking about what I already knew, rereading, and then examining the features in that section of the text. Finally, I returned to my purpose for reading and reflected on whether I had met that purpose. It turned out that I had, for the most part.

Just for this one paragraph, I tapped several skills to self-monitor while reading. Now, I am a fairly sophisticated reader, but reading this eighth-grade text was by no means a cinch even for me. Imagine how frustrated some students must feel while reading this text! My point is that we have to teach students how to pay attention to their thinking while reading informational texts—*any* texts, for that matter. They have to carry on a focused running conversation with themselves (and the author) in order to derive more than just a surface-level understanding of the text.

At first, our students may have to consistently grapple with paying close attention and figuring out what makes sense and what doesn't. Many students do not already possess "fix-up" strategies whenever they realize that the text's meaning is breaking down, and this skill requires assessment and targeted instruction by the teacher. Eventually, though, with practice, students can move toward easily identifying when the meaning is breaking down, assessing the problem they are facing, choosing from several "fix-up" strategies, and then using that strategy quickly and efficiently so they can continue reading and deriving meaning from the text. Chapter 6 details how to start the conversation about self-monitoring with students by using the "coding method" (Hoyt, 2008), discusses how to assess students' self-monitoring, and then includes suggestions for follow-up lessons.

What Does Determining What Is Important Look Like?

When we read informational text with the purpose of discovering and understanding the author's central ideas, we must determine which information in the text is critical to developing our deeper understanding of the text. We have to dig down to the sentence and paragraph levels and identify the key words and phrases that are most important in developing the author's central ideas or insights. Ideally, we can employ these key words and phrases (or similar ones) in writing a summary of what we have read.

To help students think about what it means to "determine what is important while reading," I use a "making pasta" analogy. (See the details of this analogy in the first lesson described in Chapter 7.) Most of our students have eaten pasta or are at least familiar with this food, so when you ask them to describe making pasta, they can generally give you instructions: fill the pot with water; bring the water to a boil; put in the pasta; boil for a certain amount of time; drain the water from the pasta; eat the pasta. As students share these instructions with me, I list or outline the specific steps on chart paper; and if I am working with English learners, I also bring pictures with me to further facilitate the discussion. During the conversation, I always point out the importance of draining the water from the pasta (which is a frequently forgotten step), because we do not want to eat the pasta with the water—we just want to eat the pasta!

This discussion on how to make pasta and the key importance of eating the pasta *without* the water segues into an explanation of what we do when we read to determine what is important. In any text, I tell the students, there are "pasta" words, phrases, and sometimes sentences, and the details conveyed in these words, phrases, and sentences are important to our making meaning. In a text there are also "water" words, phrases, and sentences, or chunks of text that are less important to making meaning. The author wants us, the readers, to eat and digest the *pasta* words and phrases; he or she wants *those* words and phrases to weigh in on our thinking about the central ideas and the evidence being provided to support those ideas; the author wants us to remember the taste and sensation of those words and phrases when we are summarizing and synthesizing the key or central ideas.

Let's consider examples of "pasta" words or phrases in a short book that discusses the early founding years of the United States (Finkelman, 2004). In the first chapter of the book, the author is trying to convey the idea that the national government as described in the Articles of Confederation (ratified by the Second Continental Congress in 1777) was too weak. The following text is on a two-page spread along with a painting depicting George Washington and an illustration showing various examples of paper money accompanied by short captions repeating information provided in the text (i.e., not supplying any additional information). In the excerpted text, I have underlined "pasta" words and phrases, language in the text that a small group of fifth graders (who live in the United States) and I determined were important to remember if we wanted to be able to describe and elaborate on the author's central ideas. This exercise was completed during a shared think-aloud in which we collaborated in determining what was important. Following the excerpt is a brief explanation of why we determined these particular words and phrases to be important.

Title of Chapter 1: "First Government"

Deck (the text immediately below the title): By 1783, the American Revolution was over. The United States had won. However, our <u>new national government</u> was <u>dangerously weak</u>.

Section Heading: "Too Little Power"

Text: This national government had been set up during the Revolution. It was based on a plan called the *Articles of Confederation*. The Confederation was a loose union of 13 states. In this plan the national government was weak. The state governments held most of the power. The states wanted it that way. They had just fought a war with Great Britain to escape from a strong central government.

The Confederation government had so little power it <u>could not do many of the basic things</u> a government needs to do. The Confederation government was <u>run by a Congress</u>. However, there was <u>no president to carry out the laws passed by this Congress</u>. There <u>were no courts to settle disagreements</u> between citizens or between states. Congress <u>could not collect taxes</u> and had <u>no money to pay its debts</u>.

An example of this weakness occurred near the end of the Revolution. A group of <u>army officers</u> was angry because Congress had <u>not paid them or their soldiers</u>. They were ready to march on the government and take it over. George Washington, commander of the American army, stopped them with a speech in which he appealed to their love of country.

The 13 states ignored many of the laws the Confederation government passed. There were also <u>conflicts between states</u>. Some states <u>charged taxes on things for sale from other states</u>, just as if they were imported from foreign countries. <u>Each state had its own form of money</u>. Almost no one wanted to take the "continental dollars" printed by the national government. So, farmers did not know what they could get for their crops. People with goods to sell did not know what kind of money to accept. Trade between people in different states was complicated and difficult.

Why did we underline certain words, phrases, or sentences as "pasta"? In the deck, the text just below the title that gives the reader more information about the subject of this chapter, we underlined "new national government" and "dangerously weak" because we believed the author was giving us a clue to the central idea. We planned to read further to see if other key words or phrases told us more about why our first government was not strong. When we read the first paragraph in the text, we realized the author was reviewing historical events leading up to the development of a new weak government. So, we were not reading yet about the weak first government and chose not to underline any words.

When we started reading the second paragraph and read the words *had so little power*, we became more attentive, looking for details that described how or why the government was weak. We underlined key words and phrases that told us specifically some of the "basic things" the Confederation could not do.

In the third paragraph, we noted the words *an example* and realized the author was elaborating on his point about the Confederation not being able to pay its debts. In other words, new information about what the government could not do would not be shared in this paragraph; the author was just sharing an anecdote to help us understand a previous point. We chose to underline just enough words to share this idea in a summary: *army officers* and *not paid them or their soldiers*.

After we reread the last paragraph a couple of times, we decided we needed to underline words and phrases that dealt with the problems between states because that was mostly what the paragraph was about. We were very selective and did not choose any words after "each state had its own form of money" because the rest of the information described the problems related to this issue. We felt that the issue was what was important.

You might disagree with our choices for underlining; so long as you can justify how the words you choose serve to support the author's central idea, whatever you choose is okay. We just need to be careful that students not underline too much, getting overwhelmed. I encourage students to verbally justify why they would or would not underline particular words and phrases, which helps to deepen their understanding of the author's central ideas and of the process they are engaging in to determine what is important in a text.

Consider again the words, phrases, and the one whole sentence we underlined in the excerpted text above. When I work with students, I model my thinking about not only what words I choose but also *why* I choose them. At the end of the exercise, on a separate piece of paper, we wrote a list of the phrases we underlined:

- New national government—dangerously weak.
- Could not do many of the basic things.
- Run by a Congress.

- No president to carry out the laws.
- No courts to settle disagreements.
- Could not collect taxes.
- No money to pay debts.
- Army officers and soldiers not paid.
- Conflicts between states.
- Each state had its own money.

With this group of fifth graders, we next used the list of phrases to engage in the shared writing of a summary. The students and I thought aloud about how we could use these words in sentences; then, as we composed sentences aloud, I wrote the sentences on a piece of chart paper for all to view (I explain this process further in Chapter 7). Here is what our summary looked like:

> When we first became a nation, the national government did not have a lot of power to get things done like collect taxes and pay bills. While there was a Congress, there was not a president to enforce the laws. There were also no courts in case there were problems between the states, and there were some MAJOR problems! For example, the states each had their own form of money. This was confusing to citizens who traded with people in other states.

The challenge is to gradually move the students toward determining what is important on their own. The trick is for the students to sustain this kind of close reading at the word, sentence, and paragraph levels throughout the text in order to adequately summarize the author's central ideas. The first lesson detailed in Chapter 7 (as noted above) describes how to choose a well-written text to introduce the pasta metaphor and the concept of determining what is important as well as how to demonstrate to students what the implementation of this strategy might look like.

A major roadblock to teaching this strategy is that many content-area texts are poorly written or are not student-friendly. Some potential sources cover too much information in a short amount of text, or there may not be enough prose to really determine what is important by reading closely at the sentence or paragraph level. The pasta metaphor still works with these texts, however, especially if students have had a chance to determine what is important in well-written texts. Chapter 7 also addresses how to teach with texts that are difficult as a result of overly dense content or poor or illogical formatting.

What Does Synthesis Look Like?

Synthesis can be difficult to describe to students. When students read an informational text and synthesize its content, they are able to sift through an extraordinary number of details, determining what information is important and also how this information connects to the author's central idea or theme (or multiple ideas or themes). They also come to recognize how their understanding of a topic or issue has further evolved or been affirmed as a result of this reading experience.

To introduce students to synthesis, I use the analogy of a framed photograph. On almost every teacher's desk there is a framed picture that can be used to explain this process to students. It might be a wedding photograph, or a family photograph taken at Disney World, or the framed picture of a pet. Chances are good that the students in that classroom know who is in the photograph and can share some of its details as well. Imagine a framed picture of my young daughter, Anna, and her grandmother.

If I ask my students to tell me what they notice in this picture, they might tell me that Anna is sitting in her grandmother's lap, leaning back toward her, and that her grandmother has her arms wrapped around Anna and is leaning into her. They might also add that Anna is wrapped in a lovely crocheted blanket with holes in it. Then I hold the framed picture up once again, trace my finger around the actual frame, and pose the following questions: "Why would I frame this picture? What do all of these details tell you about why I would frame this picture?" The students easily respond—it never fails—"They love each other." At this point, I announce to the students that they have just engaged in synthesizing. They have considered the important details in the photograph, used what they know about how two people can show affection that indicates they love each other, and also thought about why people frame photographs. They have engaged in this kind of thinking and reached the conclusion that I framed this picture because it shows two people I love who also share a very special relationship. The students might even venture to say that I must value that relationship if I want to capture it in a framed photo on my desk.

This type of exchange can serve as an informal way to introduce the subject of how readers synthesize information during and after reading a text. As we identify the author's central ideas as we read (and even afterward as we ponder the text further), we are all the while synthesizing. When we think about why an author would choose to group certain facts or ideas together in a text (the details in the picture, as it were) and then identify the author's central idea (the frame), we are synthesizing. Sometimes, in order to do this better, we think about other texts we have read on a similar topic or about what we are learning in our content-area unit of study that might be relevant to this. We also consider what we believe or think to be true and contrast these perceptions with the author's ideas.

In addition, at first glance, we might *think* we know what is happening in a picture on the teacher's desk. For example, consider the picture of the teacher's family at Disney World. Initially a student might say: "Oh, yeah, there's my teacher's family at Disney World. That must have been an amazing trip. I know they go on lots of trips." But if the student continues to look more closely at the picture, he or she might then notice that each family member has an arm around another family member, and the two sisters are leaning into each other with smiles on their faces, and the brother and the dad are wearing the same shirt. What the student begins to realize when he or she looks more closely is that this is a close-knit family—or that different members of the family have their own relationship and perhaps interact with each other in their own special ways. Another student might be struck by the relationship of the family as a whole and how, on the day the photo was taken, it seemed that everything was working out for them!

Consider the framed picture of a specially treasured pet on the teacher's desk. A student might say, "The dog's fur is bright and shiny as though it was just combed, and he is sitting on a big fluffy pillow. Look, he has what looks like an identification collar on his neck!" Because the student has looked closely at this picture, he or she begins to realize the dog is not just well taken care of, but actually beloved! In both cases, the student's thinking about the picture has changed, and his or her understanding of why the picture was framed has deepened. This is synthesis. When we read closely to determine what is important and why the author thinks so, our thinking may evolve or shift as we read, or our initial impressions may be affirmed. Both possibilities qualify as synthesis.

Let's take what we've just learned and apply it to the fifth graders' shared writing of the summary of the text on the U.S. government's earliest years, which we just reviewed. Something like this might result:

When we first became a nation, the national government did not have a lot of power to get things done, like collect taxes and pay bills. While there was a Congress, there was not a president to enforce the laws. There were also no courts, just in case there were problems between the states—and there WERE some major problems! For example, the states each had their own form of money. This was confusing to citizens who traded with people in other states.

The summary implies a central idea, namely, that "the national government did not have a lot of powers to get things done." What's missing from the summary is how dangerous this was. *Dangerously* is a key word the reader really has to pick up and focus on while reading the rest of this passage to synthesize and reach the deeper ideas in the text. If I wanted the students to move from just summarizing to both summarizing *and* synthesizing, I might coach instead for a summary much like the following:

> When we first became a nation, the national government did not have a lot of power, and this was a serious problem! What I didn't realize was that at that point in 1783, when the American Revolution had ended, we only had a Congress. There was no president to enforce the laws Congress passed, and some of the states were actually ignoring these laws! There was also no court system at the federal level—so, there was no way to solve problems arising between the states. The problem that popped out to me was that the government had no way to collect taxes, so it could not pay money it owed to people like the soldiers who fought in the Revolution. Plus the states each had their own form of money, and this was really confusing to citizens who wanted to trade with others from different states. Just in this short chunk of text, the author has put together enough facts to create a picture of a nation that could fall apart if it did not get its act together!

In this response, we have summarized *and* synthesized. This synthesis reveals a deeper understanding of the text than does a simple summary. In order to engage in thinking like this, all of the skills described previously are essential. Setting a purpose for reading, activating prior knowledge of text structure, self-monitoring, and determining what is important—all serve as a potential repertoire of skills (in addition to content-area-related vocabulary and background knowledge) that help us synthesize the text. Synthesizing knowledge is the ultimate purpose of the close reading described in this book.

How to synthesize during and after reading does not represent a strategy unit of study reserved for the end of the year or for after you teach the other essentials of close reading, however. Students should be introduced to the concept of synthesis from the very beginning of any kind of reading strategy instruction; then they can better appreciate the purpose of every strategy you teach for close reading. Reading is not just about self-monitoring or just about determining what is important; it is about self-monitoring *and* determining what is important *and* using one's repertoire of other skills in order to synthesize the text successfully. We must help students realize this, and the best way to do that is to talk about synthesis as part of every engagement with text.

Synthesis is not easy to teach students how to do. Many times they reveal their synthesis of the content in the text by just stating the author's central idea. That's not enough. Synthesis is more than simply identifying the central idea. It's about being able to identify textual evidence that supports that idea and being able to explain how the evidence fits together to convey that idea. It's about realizing your role as the active reader and how "thinking" is your tool for making sense of the text during this experience. This is what close reading requires, and our students can learn to do this more effectively if we are purposeful in our teaching. Opportunities to synthesize are embedded in all of the lessons described in this book. Chapter 3 focuses on introducing the concept of synthesis through interactive read-alouds and opportunities for students to write in response. In Chapters 4–8, there is a continued focus on helping students synthesize as they take on developing the particular skill highlighted in each chapter. In addition, Chapter 8 describes teaching students to synthesize *across* multiple texts as they research a particular topic to produce a short report.

In this chapter, I have suggested how I go about teaching students to read closely. As you know, the language we use with students and the methods for teaching are both key elements in enabling students to become close readers of informational text. The old paradigm for teaching with informational texts was for the students to read and learn from the text independently and then answer questions correctly. The new paradigm involves the teacher being fully engaged in an instructional cycle of assessing and teaching at the point of need. While the skills highlighted in this chapter are by no means unfamiliar to us already, these skills are too frequently taught only sporadically in strategy lessons that do not always fit together seamlessly. A major objective of this book is to describe a coherent and concise approach to teaching a particular repertoire of strategies that can be used to successfully read informational texts closely. Chapter 2 explains in some detail the critical components of this instructional approach.

CHAPTER TWO
An Assessment-Driven, Structured Approach to Teaching

The approach to teaching described in this and subsequent chapters is based on a sociocultural theory of learning that maintains that knowledge is continually constructed through social interactions. In the classroom, there are many intersections in which knowledge is constructed or meaning is being made. Whenever a teacher is thinking aloud while reading a text proficiently or is writing in the margins of a text while thinking through the text, meaning making is occurring at multiple intersections: between the teacher and the text, the teacher and the students, the text and the students, and sometimes between the students themselves. Similarly, meaning is made when the teacher guides the students in practicing a particular strategy for reading during a shared think-aloud with a group or during a conference with an individual student. A key element of these interactions is the teacher's being fully aware of the evolving needs of the students and then modeling and guiding at the students' greatest points of need.

My own preferred approach to teaching employs Vygotsky's (1978) notion of a gradual release of responsibility. Initially the teacher takes on the cognitive load of reading and thinking through the text to model for his or her students. Gradually, however, the teacher shares control of the reading and thinking with the students until ultimately they are able to work independently of the teacher. The tricky part of the gradual release process is that it does not necessarily occur in a linear fashion (i.e., the teacher models for the students, the teacher guides the students, then the students work independently). The teacher, always cognizant of the students' needs, has to engage in a dance of stepping in and stepping back to support students along the way (Englert, Mariage, & Dunsmore, 2006). This means that students may need more than one demonstration at the beginning of a lesson, and there may be several points throughout a lesson (or across many lessons) when the teacher has to "step in" and model a particular reading or writing strategy at the students' most immediate point of need. At the same time, there may be times when the teacher is engaged in modeling and he or she realizes that the students are ready to take on more responsibility for engaging strategically with the text, and in those cases the teacher needs to be ready to "step back" and allow the students to assume greater control over the meaning-making process.

The language of the discourse that occurs during these social interactions is crucial. In *Choice Words* (2004), Johnston argues that complex learning is accomplished by "powerful and subtle ways teachers use language" (p. 2). Johnston's extensive research has revealed that when working with children exemplary teachers engage in attentive listening, careful observation, and thoughtful conversations to nurture each student's identity and self-efficacy related to academic achievement. Across the school day, in a multitude of exchanges, how we engage students orally shapes how students see themselves and how they become strategically oriented independent learners. The same is true for the instruction described in this chapter in that the language you use serves to shape what students know about strategic reading, how they see themselves as readers, and what they see themselves as being able to do.

What happens when teachers and students engage in this type of learning experience over and over again? In my experience with children and young adolescents, we become a community of learners. In this kind of learning environment students can express what they already know and what they are unsure of regarding their knowledge of how to read informational text strategically (Englert, Mariage, & Dunsmore, 2006). We are a community of practice that endeavors to co-construct knowledge about reading, writing, listening, and speaking. As a result, students begin to internalize what they need to do to read, understand, and communicate effectively beyond the presence of this helpfully engaged community.

The next section of this chapter deals with what this theory of learning looks like in actual day-to-day classroom practice. Later in the chapter, I discuss how this approach meets the needs of students with learning disabilities, English learners, and students who are reading "above grade level." Chapters 3–8 go on to explore in detail how specifically this approach looks when implemented in the classroom through carefully crafted lessons.

▨ Continuous Engagement in Assessing, Planning, and Teaching

The teaching practices proposed in this book are based generally on Turbill and Bean's (2006) description of the "teaching–learning cycle" and Fisher and Frey's (2008) approach to "structured teaching." The teaching–learning cycle is continuous engagement by the teacher in assessing students' needs and planning for their learning based on those needs. When we initially assess students' oral or written work, we consider where they are at that moment in their learning and then decide where they need to go next. We then determine how they can best reach that next point in their learning and plan accordingly. As we engage in day-to-day instruction, our multiple interactions with students tell us whether or not they are learning. At the end of each lesson, we assess students' end product, and then the cycle begins again.

While the "teaching–learning cycle" focuses on the practice of ongoing assessment before, during, and after instruction, "structured teaching" focuses on how teachers gradually shift responsibility for implementation to the students themselves, that is, the practices involved in this process (Fisher & Frey, 2008). The components of this approach include: a focus lesson in which the teacher explains the purpose of the lesson and models strategic reading for students; guided instruction, when the teacher and students work together to practice strategic reading; collaborative learning, when the students work together to problem-solve, learn new information, and complete projects; and finally independent learning, when the student applies what he or she has learned to specific tasks or projects. Assessment is an integral part of this model. Assessment must occur in preparation for the focus lesson and then again during the moment-to-moment interactions between the teacher and students.

When my colleagues in the field ask about recommended approaches to teaching, I share my preference for a more detailed instructional model that makes explicit the need for continuous assessment as well as effective implementation of the gradual release of responsibility. By my definition, an assessment-driven, structured approach to teaching must include the following key components:

- Assessment of students' strengths and needs.
- Lesson preparation and text study.
- A focus lesson—explaining the instructional objectives and modeling.
- Guided practice.
- Independent practice.
- Student self-assessment.

Notice that here there are two additional requirements not specifically mentioned in the description I provided earlier. The first is that the teacher "study" the text that will be used to demonstrate strategic reading. While this process is described in greater detail later in this chapter, it is important to highlight this critical step in planning and teaching how to read informational texts closely. This step in effect requires that teachers become students themselves; in preparation for the teaching of close reading, we have to read and reread the texts we choose as the tools for learning. It is vital that we be able to articulate clearly for ourselves as well as our students our synthesis of the author's central ideas.

"Student self-assessment" is the second component of this approach to teaching that was not mentioned earlier. Students need to be actively engaged in thinking about whether or not they are being successful in reading and the specific factors that are either helping or hindering their progress. Continuous engagement in this type of reflective thinking serves to nurture each student's identity as a reader and his or her sense of agency (Johnston, 2004). You know a student has a sense of agency when he or she reveals an "I can do this" sense of self, and that is one of our ultimate goals for all students.

There is yet another component of the assessment-driven, structured approach to teaching that has still not been mentioned but should be—namely, writing. Writing about what we have just read is a powerful tool for deepening our understanding of a text (Armbruster, McCarthey, & Cummins, 2005; Headley, 2008). Writing even while we read can help us keep track of our thinking and start to determine what is important. Writing after we read requires us to consider the content of the text and/or our notes and to ponder what we really understand about this content. Students too frequently write mindlessly about what they have read, just simply regurgitating the same words used in the text. Mindful writing, though, includes considering what is important to share, organizing that information in such a way that our writing is coherent and concise, and then elaborating and revising this thinking as we put pen to paper. Figure 2.1 shows an example of the type of writing students can engage in and produce while reading closely. Writing about a text has the potential for helping us to synthesize the material accurately. Embedded in the approaches and lessons described in this book are numerous preplanned opportunities for students to write and thereby deepen their thinking. An essential element of this approach is that the teacher actually "write aloud" during the focus lessons, modeling for the students the processes a writer goes through when documenting or responding to close reading of a text.

FIGURE 2.1. A student's written response based on her notes from close reading.

■ Assessment of Students' Strengths and Needs

Crucial to the practice of assessment is the teacher's knowledge of what the students should be able to do as proficient readers of informational text. Just as important is how their development should look as they work toward proficiency. So, when we talk about a student beginning to self-monitor while reading informational text, we need to know what specifically to look for. In other words, we have to know what patterns of interaction would reveal students' growth toward close reading proficiency. Each of the following chapters includes a learning continuum for the specific skills described; with four definable stages of development in the continuum: (1) attempting, (2) approaching, (3) meeting, and (4) exceeding. At each stage, patterns you might notice in students' written work or oral comments are described. So, for example, in Chapter 6 on self-monitoring, there is a chart that describes what you might observe in a student's written work that reveals progress through the four stages toward deepening his or her understanding of self-monitoring. As part of the continuum, suggestions are included for instruction to move students in a particular stage on to the next one. There are also examples of students' work in the various stages.

A fundamental assumption underpinning the descriptions in each of these developmental stages is that students are always striving to become more proficient readers. The key is being able to describe what their work reveals and then knowing what instruction looks like that will move them forward. Thinking about students in the different stages of striving, knowing what to look for in each stage, and then being able to implement instruction to move students in each stage forward to the next one can result in powerful teaching and learning.

■ Lesson Preparation and Text Study

Just as we have to set up our students to do well, so also we have to set up ourselves to teach well. The careful selection of text, preparation of materials, and studying we do in advance serve to make our teaching easier and, as a result, our students' learning experience more rewarding.

Teachers must carefully select the text to model during the focus lesson and the text for students to read, but what you look for in a text may vary, depending on the particular strategy you are teaching. For example, when I want to teach for understanding of the features accompanying informational text, I go to the public library and pull out a stack of books related to the content area currently being studied. Then I quickly look through each book to make sure there are features (whether figures and captions, sidebars, or whatever) included and that the features are developmentally appropriate for the grade level of the students that I am teaching. When I want a core text for a whole class or small group of students to read, I am more selective, looking for a well-written text. After my students are familiar with dealing with well-written texts, then I can introduce texts that are more difficult to comprehend. The latter might include texts with unfamiliar formatting or many main ideas packed into a short extract of text. Each of the following chapters offers suggestions for locating "just-right" texts for the strategies you are teaching. Keep in mind that you are choosing texts not only for the students to read but also for you to think aloud about during the focus lesson.

In addition to selecting "just-right" texts, we have to engage in our own close reading of these texts. In other words, we have to come to know the text both inside and out to be prepared to help our students do the same. After selecting a core text for a lesson, I read and reread the text, and, as I do, I write notes about the text related to the strategy I am teaching; I have included examples of these notes in the following chapters. My notes help me design a think-aloud discourse (described below) for the focus lesson. The ripple effect of my close reading and studying of informational texts over the years is that nowadays I can read and understand how to teach a text much more quickly then I could originally. So, while this approach might seem cumbersome when you first start, this part of your preparation should get easier over time. I also keep all the texts that I have previously taught with my notes tucked away for possible later use (requiring less preparation time, as a result). In addition, you do not have to read closely every single word of text that your students will be reading. For example, your accumulated close reading experience will help you to quickly skim a text students may have chosen independently. This skill will aid you in determining how to help your students most during reading conferences with them.

Finally, preparing your materials is about more than just locating enough texts and attaching enough sticky notes and the like. Of utmost importance is creating a visually accessible image of the text for the focus lesson, when you model strategic reading for the students. To do this, you need to be able to project an image of the text on which you can write and mark in front of the students— one clearly legible to all of the students. How you do this will vary, depending on where you are teaching primarily. In the past, I have enlarged sections of the text on the copy machine and then copied it onto 11″ × 17″ paper for a small-group lesson; I have also made transparencies of the enlarged text to place on an overhead projector during instruction with a whole class. I have also placed texts on a document camera and then was able to mark directly on the text. Recently, I learned how to scan a text and drop the scanned image into SMART Board Notebook software. Then I used the SMART Board to write notes and mark directly on the text or in the margins. What is important is that the students be able to see the text while also seeing you (as the instructor) marking the text as you both read and think aloud through the text during the focus lesson. Being able to write on this image also presents a great opportunity to record the students' comments as they are offered, in the process nurturing the students' sense of identity and community.

■ Focus Lesson—Explaining Instructional Objectives and Then Modeling

The focus lesson is your first and best opportunity to catch the attention of your students. For that reason alone, it's important to state the objectives for the lesson clearly and then to engage in modeling (or scaffolding) for the students. There are two types of instructional objectives that need to be stated: content objectives and language objectives. The content objectives are directly related to the topic of the text and/or the content-area unit of study and should reflect the related knowledge and skills that students are expected to develop (Freeman & Freeman, 2007); these should correlate closely with the content-area standards endorsed by the school administration as well. The language objectives related to strategic reading, on the other hand, reflect what the student should be able to accomplish as a competent reader of informational text. For example, when I worked with a class of seventh graders studying global warming, these were the instructional objectives I posted and then explained individually:

- Draw conclusions about the causes and effects of global warming conveyed in the accompanying features of the informational text studied (content objective).
- Determine which information is most important in the accompanying features of the informational text studied (language objective).
- Explain in writing what you learned by looking closely at the features of the informational text studied (language objective).
- Describe verbally to a peer the benefits of paying close attention to the features of the informational text while reading (language objective).

Notice the verbs used for the language objectives: *determine, explain,* and *describe.* These action verbs make clear to students what they need to do to be fully engaged with and learn from the text. Examples of these objectives can be found in the lessons described in subsequent chapters.

Before discussing the next part of the focus lesson related to modeling a particular strategy, I want to reiterate that the lessons described in this book are best undertaken as part of a unit of study. This kind of teaching has its greatest impact when woven into a larger plan for developing students' knowledge and critical thinking in a particular content area. Thus, when students participate in a "reading strategy lesson" with an informational text, they are typically able to bring to this lesson certain background or prior knowledge that they have developed during other types of learning experiences. In the lessons described, reference is frequently made to opportunities to activate content-area knowledge related to the topic of the text, but sufficient attention is not paid to the numerous ways in which this can be done.

Returning now to the modeling portion of the focus lesson, during this part of the lesson I explicitly describe a particular strategy for tackling unfamiliar text (declarative knowledge), *and* then I think aloud about how I, the teacher, might use this particular strategy (or repertoire of strategies) with the core text I chose during my preparation for the lesson (procedural knowledge). Modeling (plus the conversation that ensues with the students) represents a very different process from the teacher–student interactions that might follow the traditional initiation–response–evaluation (I-R-E) pattern (Cazden, 2001). The typical I-R-E pattern would have the teacher ask, "When you read this section of the text, what did you learn about George Washington's childhood?" Then the teacher would call on a student, and the student would respond. The teacher would then follow with an evaluative comment like "right" and then move on to initiate the next part of the class discussion. While there is a place for questions like "What did you learn in this section?" this kind of interaction does not serve to teach students *how* to read a text, but only to check and see what the students understood from the text on their own.

The conversation that occurs during modeling, on the other hand, serves to make clear what students need to do *while reading* a text. This process of thinking aloud is when we make our thinking maximally accessible to students, when they get to hear *and* see what we are doing as readers with a readily accessible image of an excerpt of informational text. The key to modeling is *showing* students what we do as readers, versus merely telling them. When we model by thinking aloud about our own reading processes, we need to use *I* statements and minimize using *you* statements. Consider the differences between these two statements made by the teacher:

> Wow! Right here I was confused, and I needed to go back and reread. Let's see what happens for me when I do.

> When you get confused, you need to go back and reread.

There's something about the first statement that resonates with students more emphatically than the second statement. In the first statement, you, the teacher, are putting yourself out there as a reader for the students to observe, showing how you are vulnerable to challenging text and yet strategically oriented immediately whenever meaning breaks down. Students can readily connect with your plight because they have faced the same difficulty many times. Even when you completely understand a particular excerpt of text in your first reading, there are still genuine ways to model your thinking. Sometimes I take students back to when I was their age, saying, "If I had read this when I was in the third grade, I might have gotten stuck when I read this sentence and then decided to reread the sentence to try to make sense of what the author was saying." In this way, I am making my conversation with students more personal and furthering our developing relationship as a wider community of strategic readers. By emphasizing *I* statements, I am making clear that I am a part of this common community of practice.

Included in subsequent chapters are specific descriptions of how I have modeled my thinking while teaching lessons that use particular texts. What I find over and over again is that if the students feel a connection to what you are saying, they often want to join the conversation and think aloud with you. This is when I have to "step back" a little, but I try to refrain from moving into the I-R-E (Cazden, 2001) mode of interaction at this point. That is, I try not to start asking questions like "How did you self-monitor?"—questions that only assess and that I need to save for later. Instead, I try to conduct a dialogue with the students—that is, create a space where we are co-constructing knowledge about what happens to us as we read an informational text and what we learn as we read. Basically, we move from a teacher think-aloud to a shared teacher and student think-aloud.

While every lesson should begin with clearly stated objectives, not every lesson starts with modeling by the teacher. We may spend several days practicing a particular strategy or combination of strategies with a particular text, as there is great value to be had in practice. Think about making and decorating a layered cake, for example. If you do it only once a year, it's not particularly easy; you may even feel that you are having to learn all over each time you do it. But if you bake layered cakes frequently, making the next always seems easy. It's very much the same with becoming a skilled reader. When we teach students a new way to confront or tackle a difficult text, neurons in the brain must link together in a new way; and once linked together in that fashion, they are more likely to link together similarly in the future, creating a natural neural pathway (Fisher, Frey, & Lapp, 2008). This pathway represents "familiarity," making what you know about how to handle unfamiliar informational texts progressively easier over time. What are the implications for our instruction? Clearly, we should have recurrent conversations with students about how to deal successfully with unfamiliar informational texts as part of our content-area instruction. If students can routinely develop their own skills in tackling difficult informational texts, this "frees up the brain's working memory to formulate sophisticated understandings of what is read" (p. 37).

For the instruction that follows an introductory session, I still start out with a focus lesson. Instead of modeling, though, I spend a few minutes activating students' prior knowledge of the particular strategy I have already introduced. I want to remind them of what I revealed about my own strategic reading during a think-aloud in a previous lesson or what we revealed to ourselves during a shared think-aloud. I make sure that I'm able to project a visual image of the text I thought aloud about, with my markings and notes from the previous lesson. For example, if I wrote on the text projected by a document camera or overhead projector during the first lesson, I will project that same text with the notes I wrote. As you will notice in the lessons I describe in the following pages, I also frequently start a follow-up lesson by projecting and sharing some of the students' written notes from a previous lesson (with the individual student's permission, of course). In advance, I always preselect student notes that reveal strategic reading and content learning; as I project each note during the lesson, I think aloud or engage the students in a shared think-aloud about any elements of strategic reading and learning evident in the student's note. Again, this serves to build a feeling of community, the sense that "we're all in this together."

■ Guided Practice

Guided practice represents an opportunity for students to think through a section of informational text by using the strategy (or strategies) that you modeled during the focus lesson. They might do this alone, with a partner, or in a small group. When you coach a student or small group, you are supporting them in their achievement of a goal, but your support is clearly intended to be only temporary. The purpose of your support is to nurture students' construction of their own supports for their thinking—what we teachers call "scaffolding" for learning.

Students' responses during guided practice can be used to assess their use of a strategy as well as their comprehension of a text. After we make those assessments, we need to offer further support, and the strongest support we can offer students is carefully crafted language that has generative value (Clay, 1993; Cummins, 2011). Examples of this kind of teacher language include "Tell me more," "What made you think that?," and "What can you do to solve that problem?" We can also help a student in a difficult moment by together skimming the text at hand and engaging in another think-aloud about what we might do as readers to figure out what the author is trying to say. In the guided practice portions of the lessons described in subsequent chapters, I have included a chart that lists possible scenarios that might develop when conferring with students and suggestions for the language you might use to nurture a student's thinking and to move him or her forward.

Procedurally, guided practice involves the teacher's being fully present and knowing when to step in and step back. So, during the focus lesson, I typically think aloud about an excerpt of text, and then I assign only a segment of the text to the students to practice reading strategically. I assign just a portion because I do not want them to become overwhelmed but instead to view the task at hand as manageable. I confer with individual students for a few minutes while the others read and take notes and then regroup with all of the students to discuss what they did to understand this particular text. Next, depending on what I have observed, I then assign another (perhaps longer) section of text to the students and continue to confer with them, or alternatively I may decide to think aloud about another portion of text and provide additional support. This stepping-in and stepping-back approach gives me the flexibility to gauge students' needs, determining whether they need less or more support in making their way through the text.

Guided practice can be conducted with either a whole class or a small group. Whenever you can meet with a small group, guided practice has a more significant effect on students' engagement with strategic reading. In practice, you may choose to meet with a small group while the other students are engaged in their meaningful literacy activities, or, alternatively, you select a small group of students to work with you following a focus lesson with the whole class. Sometimes I pull together individual students or small groups based on my assessment of their work in earlier lessons, and at other times I invite students to meet me at a particular spot in the classroom if they wish to "work closely" with me. I also invite students to "guide" one another by working as partners or in groups of three. I generally do this only in classrooms where students have already done some work on collaborative conversations, or else I make sure to include some advance instruction on working together in helpful ways.

■ Independent Practice

Students need to be given countless opportunities to read and write about challenging texts without support, which is termed *independent practice*. Ten minutes of independent reading, thinking, and writing at the end of a lesson is hardly enough for a student to really take in what we are trying to teach! This is a common pitfall of instruction: students just do not get sufficient time to practice extensively what we have invested heavily in both modeling and coaching during guided practice. As a result, students stand little chance of becoming the skilled readers we want them to be, and they come up short in learning the content we are teaching in a particular subject area (Allington, 2009).

When I first started implementing 20-minute guided reading lessons with small groups of students, I vividly remember not getting to the "reading" part of the lesson until 18 minutes into the lesson! Typically, I spent too long modeling a strategy, or I let every student contribute a comment, or I let tangential conversations intervene. The net result was that not a lot of actual reading was accomplished. This scenario can also afflict longer whole-class lessons as well: I find myself giving a "maxi" focus lesson and then rushing the students to finish the text. I have tried to remedy this persistent problem in several ways—sometimes successfully and sometimes not. I plan for and implement very tightly organized focus lessons while still honoring the students' need for me to step in and step back at certain points. I also plan for a *series* of lessons (as described earlier). For each successive lesson after the first lesson on a strategy, I make sure that progressively more time is allotted for students to read. I recommend that every teacher plan for multiple opportunities for students to read, write, and talk about numerous other informational texts (that are not necessarily core texts) during the unit of study, as well.

Essential to the success of independent reading is making sure that each student has access to texts he or she can actually read (Allington, 2009). When a student is reading a text in a small group with me remaining close by for support, he or she may be able to read a more challenging text. When the student is reading a text while I am coaching a whole class of individual readers, however, it should be a less challenging text. When the student is reading independent of any nearby coaching—say, from a content-area text set on display in the classroom library—the student needs a text that he or she can read successfully without any support.

The challenge is finding texts of diverse difficulty levels that all address the same topic or subject. One idea is to work together with your colleagues to pool and then evaluate resources already available in your school for a particular unit of study. Once you evaluate what is readily available, research and locate additional texts. These may be texts you check out from the public library or find on the Internet. Primary sources accessed through the Library of Congress online can also be excellent texts for close reading. A lot of publishers in the school market have developed sets of books or magazines on the same topic or theme that are deliberately written at diverse reading levels. If sufficient funding to purchase texts is a problem, numerous grants are available through local, state, and national organizations that can sometimes be accessed for funds to purchase these materials.

It is amazing how having dozens of accessible texts for students to consult during a unit of study revitalizes your teaching and energizes your students. A few years ago, I conferred with a team of fifth-grade teachers who wanted to integrate their literacy instruction with their social studies curriculum. They decided to make this endeavor manageable and planned to meet a specific goal by establishing one instructional unit that particular school year. When I returned the following month, they had been hooked and had planned not just the one unit but were in the process of planning two more. They had assigned particular tasks to each participant and had met regularly to follow up on implementation. They had already noticed an increase in their students' motivation and engagement during instruction. The principal was so moved that she managed to locate additional funds for the books they needed and asked the team to share tips for similar planning with other teams.

■ Student Self-Assessment

Student self-assessment has to be an integral part of our reading instruction. This goes back to the idea of helping students develop a sense of agency, a sense of "I can do this" or "Wow—I did that!" To further this endeavor, we need to plan regular opportunities for students to have conversations (written and oral) about what they did to deal with a text strategically. They need to engage in conversations about what they did that worked, how they flexibly tapped a repertoire of strategies. They need to engage in conversations about what they did when they got stuck in their reading and what they need to do to continue striving toward proficiency in using a particular strategy.

I do not wish to witness students "burning out" as far as reflection is concerned. I also do not want to see opportunities to reflect tacked on to the end of a lesson as one more thing the students "have to do." So, I try to integrate reflection seamlessly into the flow of the lesson with a variety of approaches. As mentioned earlier, I may start a lesson by projecting samples of students' work from a previous lesson for the whole group to view. The conversations that follow serve as space for students to reflect not only on what their peers are doing to achieve success but also on whether they have employed the same types of strategies.

Other ways of encouraging reflection include asking students to "think–pair–share" and then to observe as they turn to talk with a partner about what they did to understand a particularly difficult passage before resuming their reading. I have also asked students to create a "plan for reading" before they begin reading a text. In this case, each student quickly wrote a bulleted list on a sticky note, placing the note next to the relevant text. As I conferred with individual students, I always started by asking him or her, "Where are you in your plan?" This query invites the student to be accountable as well as reflective.

In subsequent chapters, I put forth suggestions for helping students reflect and include some of their responses as well.

■ How Does This Approach Meet the Needs of Diverse Groups of Learners?

Students with Learning Disabilities

My first position as a teacher was in a middle school as a special education reading teacher; I was hired only 2 days before school started. I quickly found that I was in over my head as young adolescents (most of them taller than me) filled the classroom on the first day of school, many with a defeated look on their faces. They had been struggling with reading for years and did not see any way out of their predicament. They were completely unmotivated, and some were even defiant. What saved me from despondency myself was a professional development opportunity my principal offered not long after I had first met my students. I spent several days "training" on a reading program that incorporated a systematic and sequential multisensory approach to teaching reading comprehension. I quickly began implementing the program when I returned to the classroom, and my students—some for the first time in years—began to experience success almost immediately.

Then we reached an impasse. The problem was that I was using only the controlled texts from the program manuals, and, as a result, the students were only successful when they were reading the program's preselected texts. When the students left me to go to a regular education science or social studies class, their reading fell apart, and therefore they continued to be frustrated. A major pitfall of many "programs" for students with learning disabilities is a lack of teaching specifically how to bridge from the controlled texts provided by the program to the uncontrolled texts students face in every other part of their day. With my students' patience, we spent a lot of time trying to figure out what this looks like. What I realized was I had to learn how to *teach the reader* versus how to teach the program.

Let me explain. Students with learning disabilities exhibit noticeable characteristics related to attention, memory, sense of agency, and coordinated use of strategies (Reid & Leinemann, 2006). In respect to attention, they frequently struggle to stay focused on a task or a text. They may not recognize when meaning is breaking down during their reading, and even when they do, they tend to give up easily, exhibiting a lack of agency. When we confer with these students, their initial response may be "I'm done" or "I read it," not wishing to admit to their frustration right away; when we probe further, however, their response may become "I don't know what to do" or "I can't do this!" After years of perceived failure, their obvious lack of motivation only serves to perpetuate the problem.

So, how do we teach *these* readers? As noted in Chapter 1, a reader has to equip him- or herself with a variety of strategies that can help in comprehending informational text and then be prepared to monitor one's understanding while engaging in a multistep, frequently repeatable, process. Much of the student's struggle has to do with an inability to recall strategies for successful reading and an inability to engage in coordinated use of these strategies while reading (Reid & Leinemann, 2006). Instruction that focuses on making strategic reading approaches almost automatically benefits every student (Swanson & Hoskyn, 2001; Swanson, Kehler, & Jerman, 2010; Swanson & Sachse-Lee, 2000). This type of instruction possesses some or all of the following characteristics:

- Systematic, explicit explanations of strategies and steps for strategic reading.
- Strategy cuing that includes the teacher modeling or thinking aloud, the teacher explaining the benefits of using particular strategies, and the teacher prompting for the use of particular strategies.
- Segmentation, or breaking a task into smaller parts.
- Distributed practice and review, that is, providing multiple opportunities to use the strategy multiple times and over time with regular feedback.
- Dialogue between the teacher and the student that is purposeful, providing teacher assistance at the point of need.
- Small interactive groups.

These characteristics correspond well with the approach to instruction described in this chapter and the specific lessons described in the rest of this book. With my former students in mind, I would also recommend creating linkages between the classroom reading instruction and that of the special education teacher and the content-area teachers.

English Learners

The demographics underlying our classroom participants have changed dramatically during the past decade, and the chances are high that you work with English learners in your classroom. Also, the English learners in our classrooms do not always have the same language proficiencies—in either their native or home language or in English (Fu, 2009). Some students come to us with formal schooling in their native language and can achieve in content-area learning with native language materials. Other students' formal education has been interrupted in some way, and thus they do not have a strong grasp of reading and writing even in their own native language. Many students were born in our country but speak a different language at home and have not yet developed academic skills in either their home language or English. Since these students' experiences with their native language and English vary so greatly, their needs vary as well.

For these students to achieve success in either content areas or academic literacy, they need to tap into at least three areas of knowledge: their knowledge of the English language, their knowledge of the content area, and their knowledge of how to facilitate accomplishment of the tasks confronting them (Short, 2002). For example, when we ask a student to use a Venn diagram to take notes while reading a text comparing butterflies and moths, he or she has to use knowledge of the English language to understand the text. He has to make connections to his background knowledge related to insects, and then he has to figure out how to go about using this particular graphic device. In addition, English learners need to understand how to interact socially with both teachers and peers. When we ask students to think–pair–share (turn and talk with a partner) about what they included in their Venn diagram notes, this task requires some understanding of how a conversation about a text should be conducted in this particular context for learning (Echevarria, Vogt, & Short, 2004).

For students who are English learners to experience some success during the instruction described in this book, certain elements of sheltered instruction approaches to teaching (Echevarria & Graves, 2011) are incorporated into the lessons described. Sheltered instruction approaches are based on the idea that language is acquired through meaningful opportunities to read, write, speak, and listen during content-area learning. The primary ways in which the instruction described in this book serves to support English learners as well as other students include:

- Clearly stating the content and language objectives.
- Activating students' knowledge of how texts are built (as developed across the lessons in this book) and linking what English learners already know to what they are either going to learn or continue learning in the current lesson.
- Modeling for students with teacher think-alouds that include projecting visual images of the text and the teacher's notations.
- Chunking tasks into smaller segments during guided practice so they are still supported through scaffolding but also increasingly challenged.
- Using analogies to promote conceptual understanding of higher-level thinking skills such as determining what is important and synthesizing.
- Linking lessons, that is, making explicit connections between them.
- Using manipulatives and mnemonics.
- Creating opportunities to write in preparation for speaking in a small group or in front of the whole group.

In addition, the language we use with English learners is important. We have to pay attention to their language proficiency and adjust our own language accordingly. So, for example, during a conversation about the differences between butterflies and moths, the teacher might paraphrase, give examples, provide analogies, or elaborate on a student's response (Echevarria et al., 2004). This kind of language is incorporated into the examples of teacher think-alouds described in subsequent chapters and also into the conferencing scenarios and language prompts suggested for one-on-one coaching with individual students.

Students "Reading above Grade Level"

Students who "read above grade level" typically read avidly and can tell you every single detail about every single Hunger Games book, for example. They easily complete assigned reading tasks in class and always have their hands held aloft whenever you ask a question of the group. When teachers ask me how to support these students who seem to be reading above grade level and who seem hardly challenged by grade-level materials, my first response is always: "What has this student revealed about his [or her] ability to read informational texts closely? Can this student summarize and synthesize the content in these texts and across texts?"

My own experience is that there is a noticeable gap among many high-achieving students in their capacity to think deeply about a fiction text versus an informational one. They are smart or savvy enough to readily locate answers to questions in a text, fill in two-column notes and other cool graphic organizers we push their way, and complete content-area projects with poster board displays or PowerPoint presentations. But what happens when you sit down with these students to talk informally about the informational texts they are reading or writing? Frequently, they reveal to you the loss they feel when it comes to determining what is really important or to summarizing or synthesizing one text or across texts. A couple of key questions you can ask to get at how deeply the student is thinking about the text are "Tell me about what you are reading—what do you think the author is trying to say?" and then "What evidence in the text supports your point of view?" The key takeaway point is to proceed with caution before concluding that these students are really proficient in understanding informational texts.

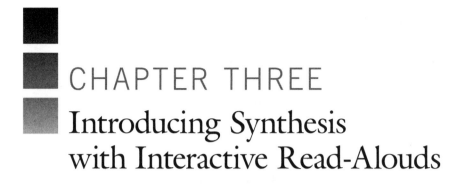

CHAPTER THREE
Introducing Synthesis with Interactive Read-Alouds

One of the easiest ways to increase students' familiarity with informational text and explicitly introduce them to synthesizing is to read aloud to them. By purposefully interacting with students during the read-aloud, we can coach them in how to synthesize the key ideas in the text. Because the text's content is made accessible (to some extent) for all learners to grapple with during the conversation, interactive read-aloud experiences also help create the feeling that all students are acting as meaning makers. Basically, by reading aloud to students, we are easing the cognitive load they must bear. Students can thus focus on thinking more deeply about the content being presented without having to worry about reading the text themselves. While there are times when a read-aloud should be just for the students' enjoyment, an interactive read-aloud can also be a great teaching and learning experience (Cummins & Stallmeyer-Gerard, 2011). In addition, students can be assigned to write a response to the read-aloud. This writing exercise should help to deepen students' understanding of the text and their ability to articulate their thinking. When students write about the central ideas conveyed in a text read-aloud, they have to actively engage in critical thinking. This includes considering what they do and do not understand about the ideas in the text and what they think about those ideas. Ideally, over time, the students should begin to read informational texts they themselves select and write responses independently as well.

▪ Consider Your Students' Strengths and Needs

What have your observations or formative assessments revealed about your students' synthesis of informational text? What are the students doing that reveals they need to learn more about how to synthesize content?

- When the students confer with you about the informational text they are reading:
  o Do they share miscellaneous details from the texts that may not relate to a central idea?
  o Do they "get" the gist of the text?
  o Do they talk about the content of the text in a way that implies real insight?
- When students write about the informational texts they have read:
  o Do they write only about the portions of the text they find most interesting?
  o Do they write about their use of strategies in a disoriented way? For example, do they shift from referring to a question to describing a visualized image without realizing how all of these thoughts help them build an understanding of the author's central ideas?
  o Do they hone in on the author's central ideas and how these ideas are developed in the text?

When considering the objective of teaching students how to synthesize the content of an informational text, it is important that we teach students to demonstrate clarity and independence in:

- Identifying and explaining the author's central ideas.
- Using the most relevant theme words in describing the author's central ideas.
- Describing the evidence in the text that supports the author's central ideas.
- Elaborating on how their thinking evolved, changed, or was affirmed.

▪ Where to Start? Explicit Instruction Employing a Read-Aloud and Presenting an Opportunity for Students to Write in Response

In the first of two lessons described below, three main teaching objectives are:

1. To formally introduce students to synthesizing informational texts.
2. To engage students in synthesizing the text while listening to a text read-aloud.
3. To model how students can begin a response to the text.

The second lesson demonstrates how you can follow up after assessing students' initial written responses. This lesson could well be implemented repeatedly over the course of several content-area units of study.

A major portion of the first lesson uses the framed photograph analogy (demonstrated at length in Chapter 1, page 26–27) to explain synthesis to students. Here's a brief review of the analogy. Consider a framed photograph on your classroom desk or somewhere at home. Visualize walking around your classroom holding this framed photograph for students to view and asking them, "What do you notice?" The students would probably try to identify the people pictured in the photograph and make inferences about where it was taken and why the people were there. With prompting, they might even note how the people were posing and the expressions on the people's faces. Then visualize what might happen if you asked the students, "Why would I frame this photograph? What do all of these details tell you about why I would frame this particular picture?" This is when the students would most likely reveal their synthesis of the framed picture as a text. The students would attempt to explain why the event represented in the photograph was important or special—perhaps even extraordinary—and worth remembering. A framed photograph is an easy prop to locate for the first read-aloud experience focused on synthesis with informational text.

Another important component, for both lessons, is the opportunity for students to write in response to the text read-aloud. In undertaking to synthesize information, having students create their own written response to a text is crucial to their thinking through and articulating what they understand about the author's key ideas. Since the students need a clear purpose and audience for this piece of writing, I ask students to write their response to the text as a letter to me. I then write or type a response back to each student describing my own thinking about the text. You might alternatively on occasion ask them to write to a peer or another educator; there are even many authors who might respond to the students as well. The best instructional method for helping students to write *highly focused* responses is to actually write a response *with* them. I describe this approach further in the lesson below. Shared writing serves to build a wider sense of community and opens a window for students specifically to see how a proficient writer (yourself), thinks when composing prose or text.

At the beginning of a lesson, I often give students blank sheets of paper so they can write *and sketch* in response to a text. I am not an artist or a graphic designer and have never modeled a sketched response myself. However, taking time to look at what students sketch without prompting or modeling can be an enlightening experience (Cummins & Stallmeyer-Gerard, 2011). I am always truly surprised by what students sketch, because they reveal so much of their thinking in these sketches—often glimmers of understanding that they were not capable of expressing in written words. The key point is to use these sketches to help assess students' synthesis of the content and then move them forward in expressing their understanding in written words as well. To find examples of students' creative use of layout and design as well as artistic representations of text content, visit my website *www.Sunday-Cummins.com*.

■ Lesson 1: Introducing Synthesis

Suggestions for Lesson Preparation and Text Study

- **Choose and study a text for the read-aloud.** See Box 3.1 for suggestions on how to select texts for reading aloud and examples of authors and titles that are particularly appropriate for read-alouds. For examples of words and phrases that can be used to describe an author's central ideas, see Box 3.2. When I am preparing for a lesson, I write notes to myself about the author's central ideas on sticky notes and write even more notes about the supporting evidence I might think aloud about in front of the students.

- **Select a framed photograph for the analogy discussion,** and think through the language you will use to explicitly define synthesis and to explain the framed photograph analogy.

- **Plan the beginning of a written response you might share with your students.** Starters might include the following:

    When I listened to [title of book], I think the author wanted me to know that . . .

    The author's central idea is . . .

    I think that the author wrote this text to reveal . . .

Be prepared to write aloud the rest of the first sentence and more, depending on the needs of your students. The response you write needs to be viewable by all students. I have written on chart paper, used document cameras and overhead projectors, and written on SMART Boards.

BOX 3.1. Choosing Informational Texts to Read Aloud

Choosing the best informational texts to read aloud can sometimes be a tricky undertaking. Following are a few suggestions for selecting "just-right" texts as well as some specially recommended authors and titles. I have also included some tried-and-true authors of trade books whose books can usually be read aloud well. You might choose some of these titles to read, or you might just use these titles as key exemplars of the kinds of texts you need to locate for your own instruction.

SUGGESTIONS FOR CHOOSING TEXTS

1. **Try to locate texts that are related to the content-area subjects you are teaching.** Listening to these texts will help your students build background knowledge they can tap into when they are engaged in other learning experiences related to that unit of study. A quick tip: first, search for specific text titles *by subject* at Amazon.com. Frequently you can read reviews of the books and often some of each book's text itself to see if it would be a good choice for reading aloud. Next, I usually go to the library in search of the titles I find on Amazon.com for a closer review of the contents.

2. **Read the text, and consider the "five *A*'s" as part of your criteria for selection.** Adapted from Moss's lengthier discussion of these criteria in *Exploring the Literature of Fact* (2003), the five *A*'s include:
   - *Authority.* Is there an author's note at the end of the book? Who is the author, and what has he or she done to develop expertise on the book's topic? In the back of Nic Bishop's books, he always describes how he researched the particular animal he is writing about and what he did to observe and take photographs of the animals. Also, when you read the text, does the author distinguish between facts and theory? Does the author cite reliable sources?
   - *Accuracy.* Are the text and visual materials accurate to the best of your knowledge? I look in the back of the book to see whether the author has included notes about organizations or other experts he or she consulted and whether other resources for further learning are listed.
   - *Appropriateness.* Are your students the appropriate audience for this text? Below, I make suggestions for choosing texts at the students' listening comprehension level and for *specific excerpts* to read aloud instead of the whole book—which makes more texts accessible to students. Another consideration is the organization of the text: is it written in a way that students will readily comprehend the author's central ideas?
   - *(Literary) Artistry.* What makes your selection an engaging text? The large close-up pictures? The use of such literary devices as metaphors, similes, or analogies? Or the mix of narrative and informational text language? These are just a few points to consider.
   - *(Kid) Appeal.* When your students listen to this text read-aloud today, will they want

you to read it again or listen to more of it tomorrow? Will they look for it in the class-room library in order to read it on their own?

3. **Make sure you are choosing *informational* texts.** Narrative and informational texts are included in the many genres referred to as "nonfiction." Narrative texts give an account of events or experiences, and the text development is normally linear, meaning the reader needs to read from the beginning to the end to make sense of the text. In contrast, informational texts typically employ a straightforward fact-sharing style and are not always linear in their development. These are non-narrative texts. Here are examples of both types of text that demonstrate my point.

- Narrative text excerpt from *Life in the Boreal Forest* (Guiberson, 2009):

  While visiting birds try to double their weight before the fall migration, the year-round forest residents prepare for snow survival.

  Chawchaw! The beavers bite into wood. Crackle! Thwak! Trees tumble. Beavers haul branches underwater to eat when thick ice traps them for months in their frozen lodge and pond.

  Hup, hup! A snowshoe hare, molting her brown summer coat into thick winter white, is desperate for a meal. After a ten-year cycle of a growing population, the forest had far too many hares and not enough food for them to eat. (n.p.)

- Non-narrative text excerpt from *Lizards* (Bishop, 2010):

  Staying safe is important to a lizard, especially when it is asleep. Many cling to the ends of thin branches. That way, if a snake creeps up, the branch will tremble and wake the lizard so it can leap to safety. If the branch hangs over water, the lizard just dives in. It will hold its legs flat to its sides and swim away like a fish. Some lizards can stay underwater for an hour. (p. 24)

- Frequently texts are a mix of both narrative and informational language. In *Kakapo Rescue: Saving the World's Strangest Parrot*, Montgomery (2010) describes the work of New Zealand's National Kakapo Recovery Team in attempting to restore the kakapo (parrot) population over time. Embedded in Montgomery's narration of the team's efforts are non-narrative descriptions of the flora and fauna coexisting in the kakapo's home on Codfish Island and the methods used to research and protect this ground-dwelling bird; she also includes sidebars with informational text on related topics.

- The primary focus of this book is teaching with informational texts that feature non-narrative language. There are a lot of good narrative nonfiction texts as well as a lot of texts that combine both narrative and informational language effectively in the same volume. Students are more familiar with narrative language, though—the language of fiction and the language they use every day when sharing anecdotes about the events in their lives—than they are with the non-narrative language of informational text. Exposing oneself to the language of informational texts has many benefits for students, including developing an ear for what this type of text should sound like when they read and write independently. When choosing informational texts to read aloud, you should just make sure you end up reading aloud enough informational texts or texts that are a blend of both narrative and non-narrative prose to help students achieve this valuable exposure.

4. **Choose texts written at the students' listening comprehension level.** Usually students' ability to understand texts they hear read aloud is higher than when individual students read and attempt to understand independently. In the beginning, you might choose shorter and less challenging texts until your students develop some stamina for listening to these kinds of texts. Plan, though, for continually increasing the complexity of the texts being read aloud. For example, in September in a third-grade classroom of one of my colleagues, we read aloud Jenkins's *Grandma Elephant's in Charge* (2003), which is written at a late third-grade level. My colleague continued reading aloud various informational texts, and when I came to visit in January I observed the students fully engaged in a read-aloud of Simon's (1999) *Icebergs and Glaciers*, written at a mid-fourth-grade level. My recommendation is not to spend a lot of time thinking about the levels of texts, but rather to just keep an eye on the rigor (and length) of the texts you are reading aloud.

5. **Plan for reading aloud *sections* of longer, more rigorous texts.** The beauty of most informational texts is that you do not have to read the entire text in order to identify the author's central ideas. As a result, we do not have to shy away from sharing a text with students simply because of its length. Instead we can read aloud several excerpts from the text. When you go to choose the particular excerpts and features to share with students, you should be guided by the author's central ideas. I read aloud excerpts from *The Prairie Builders* (Collard, 2005) to a group of fourth graders while beginning a content-area unit on the prairie habitat. Collard's central idea in this text is that, while the tall grass prairies in the U.S. Midwest have been mostly decimated by farming, there is at least one hope-inspiring community project in place to restore and conserve prairie land. The text, in a large picture-book format, is about 70 pages long. I selected enough excerpts to fill 15–20 minutes of reading-aloud time. I chose three excerpts to convey Collard's central ideas: introducing how the project began when U.S. Congressman Neal Smith located land and wrote a bill for the state to purchase the land; explaining the process for turning farmland back into prairie, including a "burn method" implemented by Native Americans to stimulate prairie plant growth; and vividly describing the flora and fauna of the restored prairie. I also selected some key accompanying features to share, including a map of the United States indicating where there were once prairies in the Midwest; photographs of scientists and volunteers growing seedlings and planting seeds; photographs showing the farmland burning process; and related captions highlighting the flora and fauna. This process of studying and selecting generally enables me to pick complex texts with rigorous contents that wouldn't otherwise be accessible if I chose to read the text from start to finish.

6. **Read from multiple types of informational texts.** While I have focused thus far on how to choose trade books to read aloud in the classroom, there are a lot of benefits to reading aloud from other types of informational texts as well, including newspapers,

magazines, and web sources. Frequently, these have just enough text to make for a good read-aloud, and they are easily accessible to students during independent reading as well. Another reason to consider other types of texts is because, frankly, there are not enough well-written trade books on every content-area unit we teach. Thus, we have to continually search for other new sources; the recommendations above apply equally to these sources of texts for reading aloud.

EXAMPLES OF AUTHORS AND TITLES TO READ ALOUD

Again, I am making these specific recommendations just as examples of authors and preferred titles that read aloud well. This list includes both informational texts and blended texts that have narrative and non-narrative language. I have divided the texts into the two main content areas of science and social studies (although certain titles, upon closer inspection, overlap both categories). In some cases, I have noted when the texts are more appropriate for the lower grades (3–5); I have included "all grades" as a category for certain texts with the caveat that, if you choose the excerpts carefully, then most texts work for the lower grades as well. For a longer list of recommended titles for reading aloud, visit my website at *www.Sunday-Cummins.com*.

Science Content

Lower Grades (3–5)

- Bang, M. *My Light*.
- Bishop, N. *Frogs*.
- McNulty, F. *If You Decide to Go to the Moon*.
- Posada, M. *Guess What Is Growing inside This Egg*.
- Sill, C. *About Raptors*.

All Grades

- Burns, L. G. *Tracking Trash: Flotsam, Jetsam, and the Science of Ocean Motion*.
- Collard S. B., III. *The Prairie Builders: Reconstructing America's Lost Grasslands*.
- Jenkins, S. *Hottest, Coldest, Highest, Deepest*.
- Montgomery, S. *The Tarantula Scientist*.
- Strauss, R. *One Well: The Story of Water on Earth*.

History/Social Studies

Lower Grades (3–5)

- Goodman, S. E. *See How They Run: Campaign Dreams, Election Schemes, and the Race to the White House*.
- Plimoth Plantation, *Mayflower 1620: A New Look at a Pilgrim Voyage*.
- Sandler, M. *Freaky-Strange Buildings*.
- Swain, R. *How Sweet It Is and Was: The History of Candy*.

All Grades

- Aronson, M. *Trapped: How the World Rescued 33 Miners from 2,000 Feet below the Chilean Desert.*
- Deem, J. M. *Bodies from the Ice: Melting Glaciers and the Recovery of the Past.*
- McClafferty, C. K. *The Many Faces of George Washington: Remaking a Presidential Icon.*
- Sandler, M. W. *The Dust Bowl through the Lens: How Photography Revealed and Helped Remedy a National Disaster.*
- Taylor-Butler, C. *Sacred Mountain: Everest.*

BOX 3.2. Theme Vocabulary, or Words and Phrases That Indicate an Author's Central Ideas

The language we want students to use when they synthesize text can generally be categorized as "themes." A theme can be considered synonymous to language that conveys an author's central idea. Frequently, central ideas are "transferable concepts," or concepts that can be applied in multiple contexts (Wiggins & McTighe, 2006, p. 74). This vocabulary is a key factor in students' being able to advance their understanding of synthesis. In the table below are "theme" words students might use for blended texts (texts that feature both narrative and informational prose) like *The Frog Scientist* (Turner, 2011), a book in the Scientists in the Field series. These texts generally describe projects or endeavors that various people have undertaken to solve a problem in the natural world. The theme words are often similar to ones that students might use in describing the central ideas in fiction. Students can be challenged further by asking them to discuss how pairs of theme words can be used to describe the author's central ideas, like *fear* and *survival* or *destruction* and *empathy*.

Words Often Used to Describe an Author's Central Ideas

• Perseverance	• Community	• Discovery
• Humanitarianism	• Global citizenship	• Curiosity
• Cooperation	• Friendship	• Empathy
• Education	• Courage	• Change
• Compassion	• Hope	• Circle of life
• Destruction	• Survival	• Communication
• Displacement	• Fear	• Dangers of ignorance
• Empowerment	• Injustice	• Knowledge versus ignorance
• Rebirth	• Oppression	• Progress
• Reunion	• Surmounting obstacles	• Role of *X*
	• Vulnerability	

When students identify themes found in informational (i.e., non-narrative) texts like Simon's (2007) *Spiders*, students can also consider central ideas revealed in such phrases as:

- The complexity and diversity of living organisms.
- The essential role of _____*X*_____ in the system of _____*Y*_____.

- Similarities/differences between concept *A* and concept *B* and why it is important to understand how they differ.
- Making the unfamiliar (or the feared) more familiar (less feared).
- Information or details about *X* presented in such a way as to transform our thinking.
- Information or details presented in such a way that we grapple with and change our thinking regarding our everyday habits and routines.
- The preordained hierarchy in nature.

Students can also ask questions likely to reveal important themes, such as:

Why would the author want us to know the content in this text? Why is this important?

What is the value of learning about . . . ?

How did the content of this text change the way I think about . . . ? Why is this important?

With older students, consider going even deeper into synthesis by moving beyond "themes" to discuss point of view, paradoxes, theories, underlying assumptions, recurring questions, and principles (Wiggins & McTighe, 2006, p. 70). These ideas are examined in detail in *Understanding by Design* (2006) and other works by Wiggins and McTighe.

Suggestions for Implementation of the Lesson

This lesson follows the approach to teaching described in Chapter 2. Plan to take at least 40 minutes to implement this lesson, even if more than one instructional period is required.

1. **Establish the purpose of the lesson.** These are the language objectives of the lesson that can be posted for students to view and/or stated aloud at the outset in student-friendly terms.

   - Listen to an informational text being read aloud, and identify the author's central ideas.
   - State in your own writing what you think the author's central ideas are, and explain why you think so.

   If the read-aloud is tied to a specific content-area unit of study, a separate content objective should also be stated, reflecting the content the students are expected to learn.

2. **Introduce the text, and activate students' background knowledge.** This is a brief part of the lesson (less than 5 minutes long), especially if the students are immersed in studying the subject of the book as part of the content focus. First, state the topic or subject of the book, and then ask the students to turn around in their seats and share in small groups what they already know about the topic; move around from group to group, checking in with each one. If you want to make this process more concrete for students, ask them to name five specific facts they are already aware of about the topic or subject.

   Next, I introduce the text. When I am studying a text in preparation for a lesson, I plan a three- or four-sentence introduction I can share with the students. For example, with the book *The Prairie Builders: Reconstructing America's Lost Grasslands* (Collard, 2005) a bleneded text which I describe reading aloud in the follow-up lesson below, I said the following:

   > Less than one-tenth of 1% of the tall grass prairie exists today. In this book, Sneed-Collard, the author, describes one group's efforts to restore some 8,000 acres of prairie at the Neal Smith National Wildlife Refuge. This project required a huge amount of collaboration and cooperation from various members of the community, and the author explains what they did to succeed.

3. **Introduce synthesis with the framed photograph analogy and a clear definition of the strategy.** After briefly introducing the text, share with the students the need to synthesize the content in the read-aloud while listening, to think about the author's central ideas, and to observe how he puts all of the facts in the book together in a way that is carefully crafted to support those ideas. Move into sharing the framed picture analogy. Some prompts you might use as you share the framed picture you chose include:

   > What are some of the details you notice in this picture?
   >
   > What else do you notice?
   >
   > Tell me more.
   >
   > Why do you think I would frame this picture?

   Segue into defining synthesis. Here's an example of what you might say:

   > A framed photograph is like a text. The author has a central idea or ideas he is passionate enough to spend time writing a book about, and to do this well he has to arrange the facts or details in such a way as to convey to the reader his central

idea. In this framed picture, you recognized what was happening and why it was important because you have chosen pictures to frame as well. Similarly, when you read a text, you use what you already know about reading and about the topic to help you understand the author's central ideas. Using that and what you learn from the text, you begin to see what the author is trying to tell you and how he organizes the text in a way that reveals this to you.

Synthesis also involves the students' response to the author's central ideas and actively reflecting on how their learning is emerging or evolving as they listen to the text. I often find that all these perspectives are too much to share in the first lesson. Follow the lead of your students and your own hunches as to their readiness to proceed. If they are at the point where you can introduce a fairly elaborate explanation of synthesis, then certainly share this type of information with them.

4. **Read aloud the text, and stop to think aloud and engage the students in a shared think-aloud.** Return to the text you introduced previously, and share the purpose for listening. You might say:

> When I read aloud today, I want you to think of this text as a framed photograph. Why would the author go to the trouble of writing this text? What does he feel is important for you to understand?

Reading aloud the text, I tend to read aloud without stopping for several minutes (so long as the students have the patience for listening that long). Whenever I stop reading, I interact with the students in one of two ways:

If the students are brand-new to synthesis, I may think aloud about what I am doing as a proficient reader regarding synthesis. For example, with *The Prairie Builders* (Collard, 2005), I might say:

> The author just shared that the construction workers bulldozed old roads and the surveyors had to plan for new ones; that Pauline, the biologist, grew seedlings in a greenhouse for the refuge; that volunteers collected and sorted rare seeds for the seedlings; and that more volunteers came to plant the seedlings. I am thinking that the author wants me, the reader, to see not only how much work is involved in restoring the prairie but also how many people are involved and how they have to work together strategically to successfully undertake a project like this.

If I had observed that the students were ready to engage in a shared think-aloud together, I might say *instead*:

> I am thinking about what we just read. The author just shared that the construction workers bulldozed old roads and the surveyors had to plan for new ones; that Pauline, the biologist, grew seedlings in a greenhouse for the refuge; that volunteers collected and sorted rare seeds for the seedlings; and that more volunteers came to plant the seedlings. When we look together at all of those details, what do you think the author is trying to tell us? And why?

As they then proceed to share, I jot their thoughts or key vocabulary words on the front board as a record of our conversation (see the next follow-up lesson, below, for how I did this with a group of students listening to me read aloud *The Prairie Builders*). The notes you take can serve as a scaffold for the students. The students can use these ideas during the shared writing experience and when they write their own responses.

5. **After reading aloud, engage in the shared writing of a sample response and in guided practice.** Sometimes it is tempting to move from discussing a text to asking students to immediately write their response to the reading. If students are fluent writers and have been writing their responses to other texts or readings for a while, this may work. If students are less familiar with writing these types of responses, however, they may naturally hesitate or be uncertain how to proceed. In the latter case, engaging students in *shared* writing is crucial. Acting to support the students (scaffold your instruction), help them to compose a sample response or at least the beginning of a response. The following prompts are helpful:

> We need an opening sentence that introduces what we believe is the author's central idea. Who can get us started by sharing an opening sentence?
>
> Why do we think that is the central idea?
>
> What details did the author include in the text to support this idea?

This is when you have to be prepared "to dance"—stepping in and stepping back as the students' needs dictate. Be prepared to think aloud, to model returning to the text and thinking through the information that might be shared. Be prepared to act as a coach, helping students try out orally what might be written, helping students to shape the right language to include in their written responses. Observe closely to determine when the students are ready to begin responding on their own. They may not be ready until after you have written the first sentence together (at first, it is all right for them to simply copy what you all have composed together). They may not even be ready to write completely on their own until after you have written a whole response together and read aloud again from the same text or a new text during a follow-up lesson.

When you do ask students to write their own responses, being fully present to coach them is also essential. In Table 3.1, there is language you might use to move students forward in their thinking and writing when you confer with them individually or in small groups.

6. **Close the lesson with conversation.** This is an opportunity for students to reflect on the content they learned from the text and on what they did as strategic readers. Prompts for reflecting on the content learned might include:

> What did we learn from this author today that is important?
>
> Why do you think so?

Prompts for reflecting on strategic reading might include:

> What does it mean to synthesize?
>
> Why is this important?
>
> How did we synthesize with this text?

As was noted in Chapter 2, there are many ways to engage students productively in reflection. If you are seeking accountability on every student's part, ask them to turn in their seat and share with their partners or ask them to jot down their response to a particular question you pose and then turn it into you, signed.

7. **Assess and plan your next lesson.** Use the descriptions of students' stages of development in Table 3.2 to help you articulate what your students are revealing as readers and thinkers. This continuum was designed after I had analyzed hundreds of students' written responses to informational text they had heard read aloud or that they had read independently. I looked across the work of many students and across individual students' work over long periods of time. I chose to make little distinction between what a third-grade student and an eighth-grade student should be able do in terms of the four-stage schema. My reasoning was that students should continually be moving back and forth through these developmental stages as they are constantly challenged with more complex texts and content as they move through the various grade levels.

TABLE 3.1. Suggestions for Coaching in Various Conferring Scenarios

Scenario/situation	Suggested coaching language and actions
The student has not yet started writing a response.	Possible prompts: • "Tell me a bit about what you are thinking." • "What are you thinking about the author's motives or reasons for writing this text?" • "Tell me more." Take bulleted notes on a sticky note as the student shares his or her thinking; paraphrase what you heard the student say by referring to the bulleted notes, and then give the notes to the student. Before leaving the student, ask the student to share aloud the first point he or she is going to make in the entry. If needed, offer to write for the student as he or she shares. Then ask the student to say out loud what he or she will write next before you walk away to confer with others. If there is no initial response, pull out the text you read aloud and engage the student in talking about the pictures. When the student begins to form an idea for a response, offer to write the beginning of the response as he or she dictates.
The student has identified the central idea but has not shared any supporting details from the text.	Possible prompts: • "What information was in the text that made you think this?" or "Why do you think so?" • Follow with "How can you write that into your response?" or "How can you paraphrase that in your response?" Be prepared to pull out the text and demonstrate by thinking aloud how you would determine important information to include in the response.
The student has stated the author's central idea in terms that are too literal.	Possible prompts: • "What do you think the author's central idea means *for you* or the rest of the world?" • "What is *one word* we could use to describe the author's central idea?" Be prepared to think aloud about how you might consider a few different words and why you might choose one in particular.
The student has written supporting details—but only in very general terms and with no domain-specific vocabulary.	Possible prompt: • "What words could you revise or change to create a *more vivid* picture for me when I read this tonight?" and "Why *those* words?" • "Let's see what happens if we change one of the words you mentioned."

TABLE 3.2. Stages of Development in Students' Written Responses Focused on Synthesis

Stage of development	Description of the student's written responses	Suggestions for follow-up instruction
Attempting	• The student simply identifies the topic of the text. • The student attempts to identify the author's central idea(s) and may include some very general evidence, but understanding the student's writing requires making additional inferences about what the student means (see, for example, Greg's response in Figure 3.1). • Drawings may reveal some understanding of the central idea in the text (with inference by the person viewing the drawing). • The student appears to be writing in a stream-of-consciousness style—where one writes as one thinks instead of organizing one's thoughts and then writing.	• After a new read-aloud, meet with this student or a small group to engage in a conversation about the author's central ideas. Give the students sufficient "wait time" to develop their responses orally. • Engage in the shared writing of a response. • Take bulleted notes as the student shares, and then give these notes to the student.
Approaching	• The student identifies the author's central idea, though perhaps in a way that does not get at the larger underlying idea. • The student includes some general evidence to support the central idea but may not fully recognize it as evidence, requiring the teacher to infer the student's meaning. "General" evidence implies references to details in the text in more general terms rather than domain-specific vocabulary and/or particular facts (see, for example, Juliana's response in Figure 3.2). • The student may include some elaboration but does not make clear how the elaboration serves to reveal the connections between the evidence and the central idea. Elaboration (as detailed in "meeting," below) may have an "attached" or "tacked-on" quality. • The student uses some theme words (like *perseverance* and *courage*) in describing the central idea(s), but not necessarily in a way that conveys true understanding of the terms being used. For example, the student may use a word that the teacher wrote on the board during the group discussion of the text—a word that he or she does not yet fully understand but is still attempting to come to terms with. • The student's drawings create more clarity of what he or she is trying to convey in the written response.	• See recommendations for "attempting." • List domain-specific vocabulary on the board for the whole class to view. Meet with this student and ask him or her to share some of the specific words he or she plans to use and why. Write these words on a sticky note, and give it to the student. • After a read-aloud, meet with a small group of students (ones evidencing the same need) to practice articulating orally what the first sentence in their entry should be. • When the student shares his (or her) response with you, prompt him to suggest a place in the response where he might have usefully elaborated with additional details. Remind her (or him) how to use an editing carat to add in a sentence or two or how to draw an arrow to the bottom of the entry to indicate that she wants to elaborate further.

(cont.)

TABLE 3.2. *(cont.)*

Stage of development	Description of the student's written responses	Suggestions for follow-up instruction
Approaching *(cont.)*	• Some organization or natural flow is evolving in the student's writing, but most of the response is stream-of-consciousness writing.	• During a mini-lesson, share examples of students' responses that are well-organized; engage the students in a shared think-aloud about how well the sample student responses are organized and how they could be improved.

Meeting	• The student identifies the author's central idea, also supplying supporting evidence from the text. This central idea has a thematic quality to it.
	
	• The student elaborates on how the central idea and supporting evidence are connected (i.e., how the evidence supports the central idea). This may still require some inference by the reader, but it is easily accomplished (see, for example, Maddie's response in Figure 3.2).
	
	• Elaboration (as deemed developmentally appropriate) may include but is not limited to:
	  o Reference to the author's overall text structure (such as compare–contrast or cause–effect).
	  o How the student's thinking changed from the beginning to the end of the text, or at what point the student's thinking changed.
	  o Connections to the student's own ideas or experiences or other texts he or she has read; and examples from other world events or other scenarios shared as similar to or contrasting with the author's central idea.
	
	• Elaboration has a mostly integrated quality. The student's ideas are woven into the explanation of the author's central ideas and the supporting evidence cited in the text.
	
	• Depending on the context for writing (e.g., timed writing, writing by hand, or composing/revising on the computer with plenty of time), the written text is organized in a mostly coherent way, and the teacher can clearly see the flow of the student's logic and understand the student's ideas.
		• Read aloud or ask the student to read independently more challenging texts.
		
		• Model thinking aloud about several central ideas found in the text.
		
		• Model connecting global themes to the author's central ideas.
		
		• Engage in a shared analysis of good examples of students' responses that are well organized and where the flow of ideas is clear and straightforward.

Exceeding	• The student's explanation of the central idea(s) moves beyond the text to global themes, including both evidence from the text and evidence from beyond the text that elaborates on the themes. • The student's elaboration is similar to that at the "meeting" level, but it seems surprisingly insightful and novel in some way.	• See the recommendations for the instruction of students who are "meeting" expectations. • Introduce the student to elements of persuasive writing (in grades 3–5) and argumentative writing (in

(cont.)

TABLE 3.2. *(cont.)*

Stage of development	Description of the student's written responses	Suggestions for follow-up instruction
Exceeding *(cont.)*	For students in grades 6–8, an "exceeding" response normally includes elements of argumentative writing (Toulmin, 2003), for example, a student making a wholly original claim and then providing evidence from informational texts and an explanation of how the claim and evidence are connected (i.e., a warrant) (Hillocks, 2012). The student might also allude to certain qualifications and/or counterarguments. An example of a claim by a student writer might be "When humans change or destroy habitats, the consequences can be disastrous for the local wildlife," and evidence from multiple texts (among other possibilities) could be used to support this claim.	grades 6–8) as different ways of interacting with and responding to global themes explored in many informational texts.

When you use the continuum to assess a student's work, you might notice characteristics from more than one stage or level. The object is not to decide for certain which developmental stage a student's work falls into, but rather how to move the student forward by considering where he or she is now and how best to enable that child to grow from this point forward. The descriptions in the table are in no way exhaustive or final. Consider this schema as a potential starting point for your own practice, as a dynamic tool that you can change and revise as you analyze your own students' responses and as they grow in their ability to respond to texts.

For each of the four developmental stages in this continuum—attempting, approaching, meeting, and exceeding (expectations)—Table 3.2 presents examples and analyses of students' work and suggestions for follow-up instruction designed to move them forward in their learning.

Examples of Students' Written Responses

The students' written responses shown in the remainder of this chapter were produced during an introductory lesson with a group of fourth graders who were studying animal habitats. The teacher and I had previously discussed how important it was for students to realize what happens when animal habitats are changed by humans in certain ways, and this conversation helped me decide what text I would read aloud to the class. The lesson included introducing the framed photograph analogy, defining synthesis, and reading aloud *The Wolves Are Back*

(George, 2008). This book is about what happened to the flora and fauna in Yellowstone National Park when wolves were hunted to extinction in the lower 48 states by 1926. George also describes what happened when the wolves were later reintroduced into the park again in 1995. The central ideas are that the wolves once played an important role in the ecosystem of Yellowstone, and there are significant and sometimes unforeseen consequences when humans change the features of an ecosystem. While these students had previously written responses to fiction texts that were read aloud by the teacher as well as independently by the students, my lesson marked the first time they wrote responses to an informational text that was read aloud.

In Figure 3.1, which presents an example of an "attempting" stage response, Greg's writing reveals some grasp of the author's central ideas in his statement "I think the animals will not eat if it wasin for the wolves." He seems to realize that the wolves are important to the survival of the other animals and appears to understand that there is a cause-and-effect issue at hand.

How could we move Greg forward in his learning during the next lesson?

- To encourage a clearer explanation of the author's central idea, meet with him one-on-one and ask him to share orally what the first sentence of his new written response will be—a sentence that clearly states the author's central idea. Coach Greg in shaping his thinking orally, and then ask him to repeat the sentence a couple of times before writing it down.
- To encourage Greg to include supporting evidence from the text, meet with him one-on-one and write bulleted notes on a scratch piece of paper while Greg shares. Then, give him your notes to refer to when writing his response.

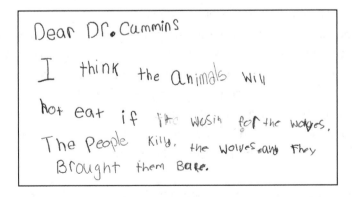

FIGURE 3.1. Example of the *attempting* stage (Greg's response).

In Figure 3.2, Juliana has made a very literal interpretation about the author's central idea, as revealed in her statement that "the wolf's in the book were gone, and when they came back, they helped." The reader of Juliana's response has to infer to some extent that the return of the wolf population to Yellowstone National Park had a positive impact on the other species inhabiting this area. Juliana includes some supporting evidence from the book, but only in very general terms, like "they helped a lot of animals build homes again." She has synthesized the information by grouping together facts from several points in the text. She describes how animals that were formerly kept in check by the wolves began to proliferate unduly and, as a result, destroy the habitats of other animals: the elks ate the grasses that Vesper sparrows normally used for nesting material, the buffalo trampled the young aspen trees the flycatchers lived in, and so on. Her final statement about the wolf she spotted at her cousin's house was an attempt to connect all of what she had learned to her own experiences. She might not have had the background knowledge to do this successfully, but her attempt nonetheless could be built on in future lessons.

How could we move Juliana and others with similar responses forward?

- To make sure she is grasping enough of the domain-specific (i.e., content-area) terms (like *elks, Vesper sparrows,* and *aspen trees*) from the read-aloud to incorporate them into her writing, read the text aloud again, and walk back through the text with the whole class or a small group, and then list the key new vocabulary words on the board for them to refer to while writing.
- To enable Juliana to make a clear statement about the author's central idea at the beginning of her response, engage her and a small group of students with similar needs in *shared writing* of an introductory sentence when they start a new response. Then they can use this sentence to start their own response or write a similar one of their own.
- To encourage Juliana to gather supporting evidence in the text, moving from the general ("animals build homes") to the specific ("Vesper sparrows build nests"), engage her in a one-on-one conference where she shares her thoughts orally (with prompting as needed). Take bulleted notes on a sticky note and leave it with her to use when she writes. Later, with her permission, use her first response and her new response (with more specific details) as a mini-lesson for other students to consider.

In Figure 3.3, Maddie's written response is somewhere between meeting and exceeding my expectations for a first lesson. She identifies the text structure of cause and effect (which I did not explicitly state in my introduction to the text,

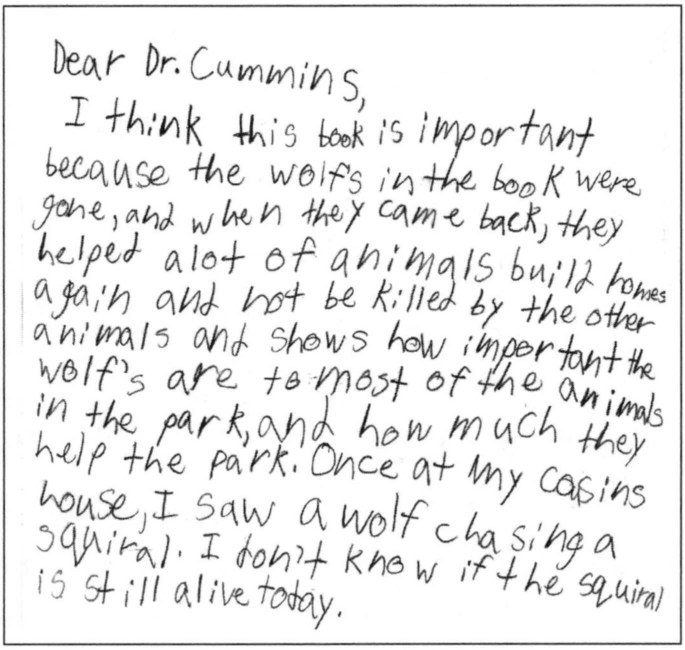

Dear Dr. Cummins,
I think this book is important
because the wolf's in the book were
gone, and when they came back, they
helped a lot of animals build homes
again and not be killed by the other
animals and shows how important the
wolf's are to most of the animals
in the park, and how much they
help the park. Once at my cosins
house, I saw a wolf chasing a
squiral. I don't know if the squiral
is still alive today.

FIGURE 3.2. Example of the *approaching expectations* stage (Juliana's response).

though I wish I had). She identifies the central ideas in general terms ("to show children [cause and effect]") and in more thematic terms ("the food chain was off [balance]" and "when the wolfs were gone, everything was out of order"). She identifies general evidence ("some animals came [back] and some left" and "then everyone saw that we need wolfs"). Her example of "when your mom isn't [there]" is insightful, helping to elaborate further how all of the details are connected. She also states how her thinking changed as a result of this book. Her use of exclamation marks and underlining emphasizes certain points, and reading this response is almost like listening to her talk to you; she clearly exhibits passion about what she has learned. *What's missing* are the details from the text that support Maddie's ideas.

How could we move Maddie and others with similar responses forward?

- To encourage Maddie and others to provide supporting textual evidence, engage the students in an analysis of several students' responses that include supporting details.
- After reading aloud a new text and having a discussion about the author's central ideas, engage the students in shared writing of a list of the evidence in the text that supports these ideas. Encourage them to use this list as they compose a new response.

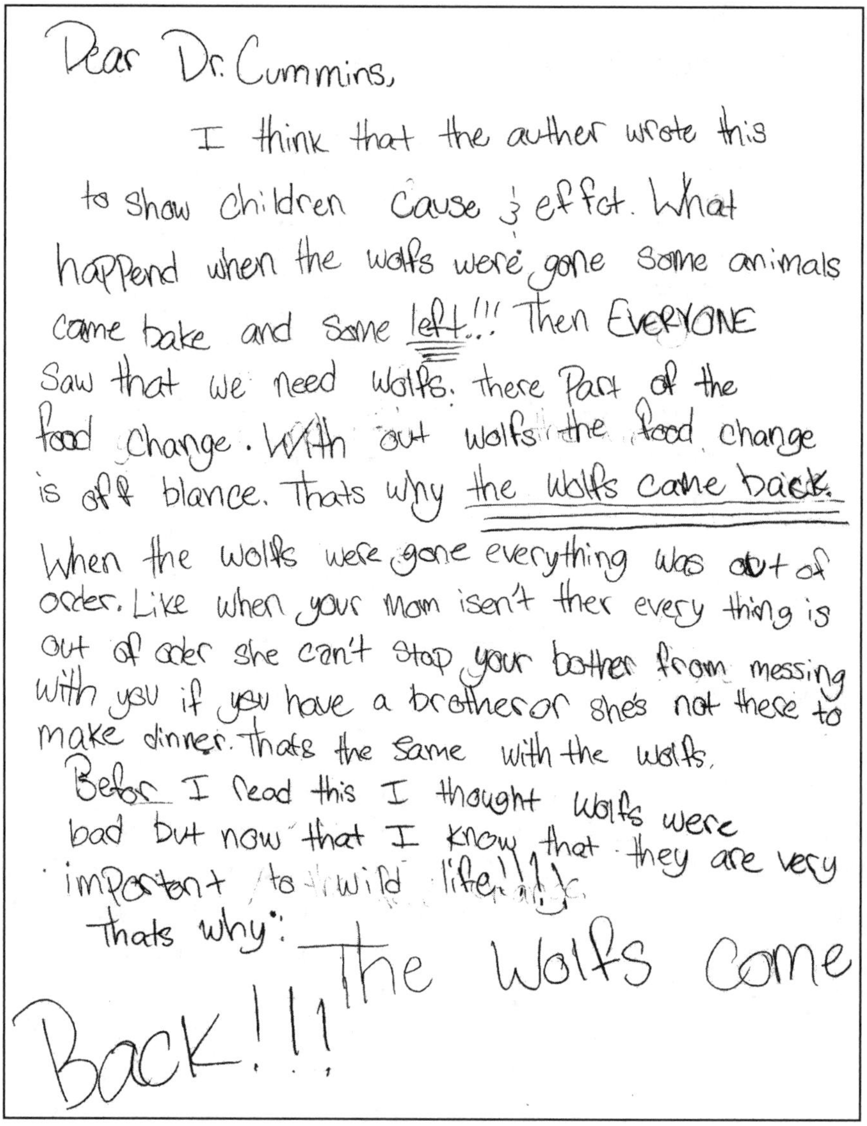

Dear Dr. Cummins,

    I think that the auther wrote this to show children cause ; effct. What happend when the wolfs were gone some animals came bake and some left.!!! Then EVERYONE Saw that we need wolfs. there Part of the food change. With out wolfs the food change is off blance. Thats why <u>the wolfs came back.</u>

When the wolfs were gone everything was out of order. Like when your mom isen't ther every thing is out of oder she can't stop your bother from messing with you if you have a brother or she's not there to make dinner. Thats the same with the wolfs.

    Befor I read this I thought wolfs were bad but now that I know that they are very important to wild life.!!! Thats why: The Wolfs Come Back!!!

FIGURE 3.3. Example of the *meeting to exceeding (expectations)* stage (Maddie's response).

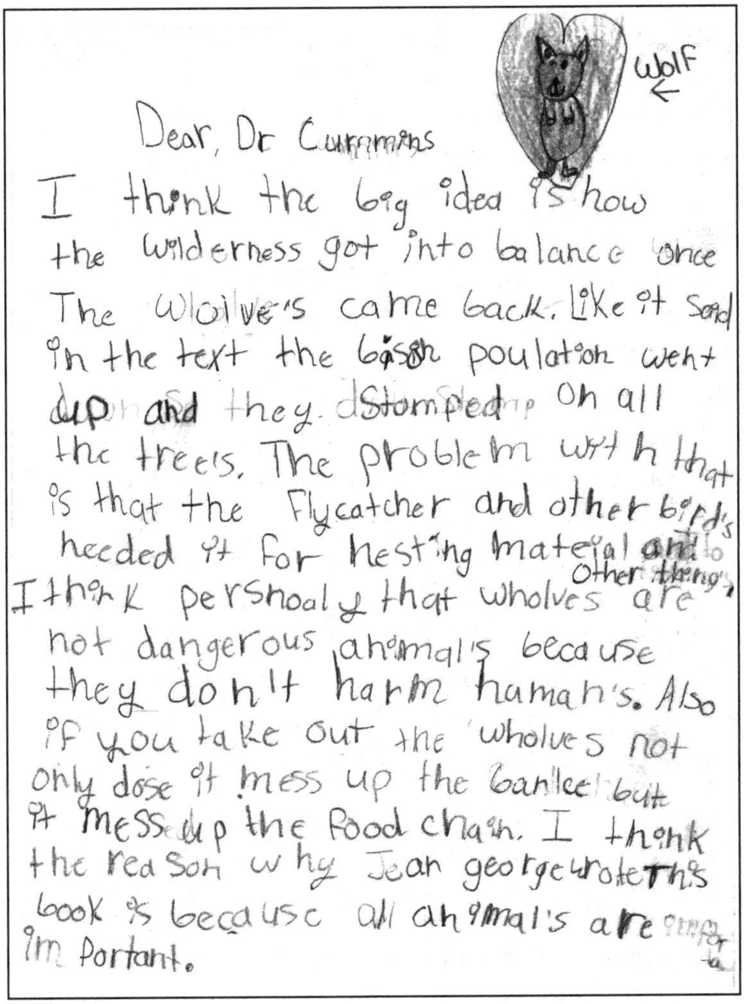

FIGURE 3.4. An example of exceeding expectations (Katelyn's response).

■ Lesson 2: Using Students' Written Responses to Nurture Their Thinking

Assessing and Planning

A lesson was arranged with this same class of fourth graders on the day after the first lesson. Before this follow-up lesson, I looked through the students' responses. The students were clearly getting the gist of George's (2008) text, but they needed some additional help in the following three areas:

1. Using domain-specific vocabulary or more-detailed terms to describe the various animals and habitats.
2. Using specific details from the text.
3. Using theme-related vocabulary words to identify the author's central ideas.

I went back through the students' responses and chose two entries to share at the beginning of the lesson the next day. One was Maddie's (shown in Figure 3.3), and the other was Katelyn's written response (see Figure 3.4).

Much like Maddie in her written response, Katelyn gets at the central idea in the text and shares how her thinking changed as she synthesized the content of George's book. Unlike Maddie, Katelyn includes specific supporting details from the text to support her point ("Like it said in the text the bison [population] went up and they stomped on all the tree's. The problem with that is that the flycatcher and other birds needed it for nesting material and other things"). I chose these entries because the students evidenced some synthesis of the material on their part and also elaborated on the author's central idea. Katelyn also included textual evidence with domain-specific vocabulary. Their responses could serve as mentoring texts for their peers.

Implementing the Follow-Up Lesson

To begin the second lesson, I reviewed the framed photograph analogy and definition of synthesis, and then I shared the two entries with the class. I kept my points to a minimum, posting a copy of Maddie's entry for all of the students to view by using a document camera. Then I shared aloud with the students that when I read Maddie's entry I had a clear idea of the central idea in George's book. I asked the students to share specific words, phrases, and sentences from Maddie's entry that revealed to me her thinking about the central idea; as they identified the words and phrases in Maddie's writing, I underlined those. We also discussed her analogy to what happens when a mother is not at home. We talked about how Maddie went beyond the text to elaborate on her thinking. I followed by posting a copy of Katelyn's response and started again by affirming that she too had written about the central idea. As with Maddie's response earlier, I then asked the students to notice the specific details she shared as evidence in the text. I encouraged them to notice such words as *bison* and *flycatcher*; when they did, I underlined those words for them to view. In closing, briefly, I made the point that the reader could visualize what Katelyn was saying because of her use of specific words like these instead of more general words like *animal*.

Following this short conversation, I next read aloud from *The Praire Builders* (Collard, 2005). As noted earlier, I had three goals in mind during this interactive read-aloud, based on my analysis of students' responses to *The Wolves Are Back*. First, there was the lack of domain-specific vocabulary (i.e., they referred to "animals" and "plants" instead of "elks" and "aspen trees"). As I read aloud from *The Prairie Builders*, I would stop and reread sections that had important new vocabulary words like *biologist* and *environment*, and then we would list those words on the board. Second, I also wanted the students to remember the details to include in their responses, so I stopped at key moments and asked the students to repeat to their partner the events that took place to restore the prairie. Finally, there were very few of what I call "theme vocabulary" words used in the first set of responses; so, I also engaged the students in discussing words that would describe the project to restore the prairie. The project Sneed chronicled took a tremendous amount of long-term work by many people, so I introduced the word *perseverance* and wrote it on the board. With these points in mind, I read-aloud and interacted with the students for about 20 minutes and then asked the students to write their own response during the final 25 minutes that were available for the lesson.

Analysis of Student Responses after the Follow-Up Lesson

Many of the students' second responses were more thoughtful about the central ideas in the text and included more textual evidence as well. Take a moment to compare Jasmine's response to *The Wolves Are Back* (Figure 3.5) with her response to *The Prairie Builders* (Figure 3.6), written after the second lesson. Notice that in Jasmine's first response she identifies the central idea in very literal terms—"so that people can understand how important wolves are to the wilderness." Her response discusses mostly central ideas in the text, and the evidence is stated in general terms—"Wolves help other animals live." The caption under the picture of the wolf pup does include more specific details than are shared in the body of the entry ("Wolves help the birds to get grass for food and nesting materials by keeping the elk population down").

As with her first response, in the second response Jasmine shares a central idea (still in very literal terms)—"we need to bring back the [prairies]." Unlike the case in her first response, she then shares why: "so that children can see what their land was once." She also goes on to touch on three ideas in the text. With some

Dear Dr. Cummins,
I think the author wrote this story, so that people can understand how important wolves are to the wilderness. Wolves keep the wilderness balance. Wolves help other animals live. I also think the author wrote this story to tell people that wolves aren't always dangerous. They don't always harm people.

Wolves help the birds to get grass for food and nesting materials by keeping the elk population down.

Wolves aren't that bad or dangerous. They are actually good for nature.

FIGURE 3.5. Jasmine's written response during the first lesson.

inferences required by the reader of her response, Jasmine nonetheless conveys that the animals disappeared when the prairie was destroyed and "we need to get them [the animals] back." She follows with her personal reaction to this state of affairs. Then she moves on to address the number of people it took to restore the prairie—being very specific in her choice of words—and shares her surprise at this. She also discusses how her thinking about the burn method shifted. She closes with her hope "that once more the prairies will be back." There is a natural logical flow as Jasmine first relates the author's ideas and then integrates her own reactions to those ideas. She is now ready to be instructed on how best to break these ideas up into paragraphs and how to develop her thoughts further—particularly with additional evidence from the text to support her own points and the use of domain-specific vocabulary to describe evidence from the book.

In addition to Jasmine, Katelyn wrote a deeper response to Collard's *The Prairie Builders* as well. Take a moment to read her response below, and to look at her drawing (in Figure 3.7).

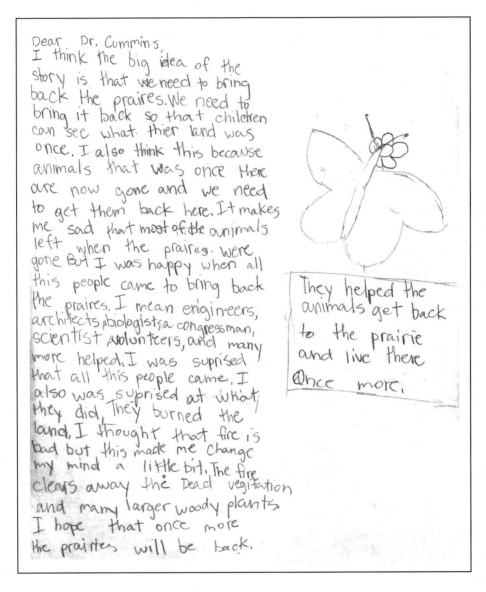

Dear Dr. Cummins,
I think the big idea of the story is that we need to bring back the praires. We need to bring it back so that children can see what thier land was once. I also think this because animals that was once here are now gone and we need to get them back here. It makes me sad that most of the animals left when the praires were gone But I was happy when all this people came to bring back the praires. I mean engineers, architects, biologists, a congressman, scientist, volunteers, and many more helped. I was suprised that all this people came. I also was suprised at what they did, They burned the land. I thought that fire is bad but this made me change my mind a little bit. The fire clears away the Dead vegitation and many larger woody plants. I hope that once more the praires will be back.

They helped the animals get back to the prairie and live there once more.

FIGURE 3.6. Jasmine's written response after the second lesson.

Dear Dr. Cummins,

I was a little surprised at the beging [beginning] I tough [thought] they were burning the prairie for a bad reason but torw's [toward] the end I realized they were good people. Especialy [Especially] the coungrass man [Congressman] I thank him so much for helping are [our] earth. He search [searched] 6 years to find a praie [prairie] it took perseverance to so [do] somethink [something] like that it [is] just amazing. I think the government and everyone on earth sould [should] help the environment more. So realy [really] the true meaning of this story is help the earth try try again never give up in what you belive [believe] is right. Like it said in the "The Wolves are back" humans can mess up one large national park imange [imagine] how much they can mess up are [our] earth and how much they can do good to the environment. The congress man [Congressman] is a wonderful example of a human who is help's [helping] are [our] earth. I'm not saying go plant a whole entire praie [prairie] even thoug [though] that would be nice. Recycle, turn the sink off, take sort [short] showers these thing [things] can help animals plants and even humans.

—Katelyn

Unlike her response to *The Wolves Are Back*, Katelyn's written response this time includes thinking that moves beyond the text. She elaborates on the central idea that we all need to help the planet Earth in some way (just as the Congressman did), but she also demonstrates how she has thought this through. She reveals that she has realized that not all of us can "go plant a whole entire prairie." She offers alternative ideas, tapping what she knows about how we can help the Earth. She makes suggestions like "recycle, turn the sink off, take [short] showers." Her drawing of a prairie burning with a ban sign is linked to the beginning

FIGURE 3.7. Katelyn's drawing in response to *The Wolves Are Back*.

of her response; when she first heard about the biologist and her volunteers burning the farmland to begin the restoration project, she thought this was wrong. Her second drawing shows how her thinking changed as she listened more closely and realized the biologist was just using a traditional Native American method for stimulating the growth of prairie plants. Katelyn's response still needs some work, particularly in the areas of spelling and editing, but given the context of writing on demand for 25 minutes, this response reveals higher-level thinking about the central ideas in the text.

Of course, not every student does this well this early. There were some students whose written responses totally lacked coherence and a few others who misunderstood the concepts presented. For example, Carolyn wrote in her first sentence, "I think the author's main idea was to tell us that you don't need machines to make a difference." Actually, there were a lot of machines used to improve the land in the prairie restoration project. Some students identified and elaborated on the central idea but were unable to share any supporting evidence from the text. Others shared evidence, but only in very general terms. Finally, one student managed to write only one sentence during the 25 minutes available for the writing exercise.

What I realized as I carefully read the students' responses after the follow-up lesson was that we were very much at the beginning of the journey. At the same time, though, I smiled as I read the bits of wisdom they conveyed even as they struggled to get their thinking down in print. Leah wrote, "I think the book was telling me about believing in your dream and to not give up." Jake shared, "I would help all I could to keep the prairie there because I don't think we could manufacture something like that again." And Kelsey exclaimed, "This book was great to read when you're going green!"

With this class of students, I would continue to share their responses during mini-lessons and to read aloud in a purposeful, interactive way that included highlighting the author's central ideas, writing key vocabulary words on the board, and discussing supporting evidence. I would also engage in shared writing of responses after the read-aloud, where we would write a response together for all to view. This would give me an opportunity to demonstrate specifically how to include supporting evidence with specific vocabulary, how to divide ideas into paragraphs, and much more. Finally, I would also begin to ask the students to self-select informational or blended texts for independent reading and for writing in response to a different part of the content-area unit of study or during another part of the day.

◼ What's Next?

This chapter mainly dealt with helping students to understand the main text in a book—the prose, or running text—without explicitly addressing the special features, boxes, or sidebars an author might also include to support or extend the ideas in the main text. Chapter 4 describes how to engage students in paying attention to these types of "features" and in thinking about how the main text and these features work together to convey the author's central ideas.

CHAPTER FOUR

Understanding the Features of a Text

Unlike the situation a generation ago, informational text for children and young adolescents nowadays is redolent with features that may include maps, boxed commentary or highlights, diagrams, photographs or illustrations with captions, timelines, and much more. The features of informational text are the elements that help the reader navigate the text like a table of contents, titles, and subtitles as well as the elements of a text that provide additional content to support and develop the ideas in the running text like maps, diagrams, photographs, illustrations, and captions. Together, the features and the running text *are* "the text," meaning that one cannot serve to convey the author's central ideas without the other. So it is essential that students pay attention to the content in both the text and the features. While many students can practically close their eyes and locate the table of contents or photographs with captions, they cannot always clearly articulate what they have just learned after examining a particular feature closely. Many students tend to treat the features as purely supplemental to the text, perusing them quickly and often solely for their aesthetic appeal. They might say to you that the pictures in a text are "really cool," but they cannot necessarily explain how they helped them understand the running text better. What is lacking is students' full realization that a text's features contribute a great deal to the meaning of the text and support the readers in many ways as they read a new or unfamiliar text.

■ Consider Your Students' Strengths and Needs

What have your observations or formative assessments revealed about your students' use of the features accompanying informational text? What have you observed that indicates they need to focus more closely on the specific information contained in the features of a text?

- When students confer with you:
  - Do they talk about the content of the text but not any of the features?
  - Do they talk about the appeal of a particular feature ("That's a cool picture!") but not about what they learned from the feature?
  - Do they share what they learned from a feature but not necessarily how that helped them understand the main text or the author's central ideas?
  - Do they integrate what they have learned from the features and the main text into a discussion about the author's central ideas?
- When students write about the features in a text:
  - Do they write solely about the content expressed in the running text, or prose?
  - Do they write about any features at only a surface level of understanding?
  - Do they write about one part of a particular feature in a way that reveals a misunderstanding of the author's ideas (e.g., writing about the illustration or photograph but not about the caption)?
  - Do they write fluently about the author's ideas, drawing from the content in both the accompanying features *and* the main text?

If our objective is to teach students how to properly understand the features included in an informational text, it is imperative that we show them how to demonstrate independence in:

- Noticing and being able to identify the various features.
- Comprehending and paraphrasing the actual content of the features.
- Making connections between the content of the features and the ideas in the text in order to better synthesize the two.
- Assessing the author's use of features and evaluating how they may convey other perspectives.

■ Where to Start? Explicit Think-Aloud and Modeled Note Taking

Two lessons are described in this chapter, each of which could easily have been expanded into a series of lessons based on the needs of your students. The first lesson focuses on having students develop an awareness of particular features as well as be able to articulate what they learn from those features. The second lesson provides an example of how you can begin teaching students to synthesize both the information gathered from features *and* from the main or running text. This lesson is important because, when we ask students to write their response to an informational text, they do not always readily integrate what they have learned from the text's accompanying features into their response. The students need to understand that features contribute a great deal to the meaning of the text and support the reader in highly significant ways in making sense of the text as a whole.

My suggestion would be to incorporate these two lessons into a 3-day cycle of lessons that would occur at least once during each content-area unit of study. The cycle would likely be:

- Lesson 1: Introduction or review of the purpose of one or two particular features.
- Lesson 2: Guided practice in strategically reading a two-page spread of text, including the same features discussed in the preceding lesson.
- Lesson 3 (optional): Additional guided practice and then independent practice with the same or related features.

Table 4.1 highlights the purposes of the features most commonly found in short texts like magazine articles or selected sections in a textbook (it deliberately omits features found only in longer texts, such as the table of contents, glossary, and index). Essential to effective instruction in reading is our ability to clearly articulate to students the specific purposes of the features that accompany text. Because many of these features are complex, however, we must always be able to explain to students the potential pitfalls in trying to understand them. I have tried to highlight both as in the table.

Features are more easily taught when encountered in use rather than in isolation. As the Table 4.1 discussion of maps makes clear, the information imparted by these features sometimes supports the content *of other features* as well as the

TABLE 4.1. Features Commonly Found in Shorter Texts and Their Purposes

Feature	Discussion of purpose
Titles	The title usually indicates the topic or subject of the text, but it may occasionally just allude to the topic. Readers use the title to begin making predictions about what they will be reading.
Deck	Many short nonfiction texts include a "deck," or brief introduction to the article or chapter. Typically set in a different font or color, the deck is positioned between the title and the beginning of the main text or the first section heading. The purpose of the deck is to give the reader more information than the title and also to attract additional interest. Frequently the deck's wording speaks directly to the reader, posing a question or providing just enough information to tantalize the reader and to make him or her want to explore the text further. Here's an example of a deck from an article titled "Storm Warning" (Brooks, 2010): *Supersized thunderstorms rumble. Lightning slashes the sky. Hurricane-force winds blow. Deadly tornadoes spin. Welcome to the central United States, the stormiest place on Earth.*
Headings and subheadings	Running text is typically broken up into sections, each with its own heading. There may be a single level or multiple levels of headings, some of which may be designated as "subheadings." Regardless of the format used, headings clue in the reader as to what the author will be addressing next in the text. Sometimes the heading may seem crystal-clear, such as with "First Battle with the British." At other times the heading may seem less clear to students and perhaps only allude to the content. Sometimes authors use idioms in headings, which can be highly confusing to certain students, especially English learners. It is important that readers notice whether headings are providing useful hints of the information being imparted to readers in the text's respective sections.
Photographs and illustrations	Photographs and illustrations provide visual information to the reader. The information provided by these visual aids normally supports the ideas presented in the running text. Sometimes this information extends these ideas by presenting additional or multiple examples. Your students should always be able to distinguish between a photograph and an illustration. In certain texts, illustrations may be sketches, drawings, or paintings rather than photographs, particularly when (as in history texts) the period being covered predated cameras. Sometimes younger students may not realize that the drawings are depicting the distant past, leading to a temporary confusion on their part.
Captions and labels	Captions describe the photographs or illustrations, providing readers with more information than they could have assimilated solely from the figures alone. For example, a caption might include the name of the species of the deer featured in the photograph. Labels included within figures, diagrams, and the like serve a similar purpose (e.g., naming the specific organs featured in an illustration of the digestive system). Of course, since a picture "is worth a thousand words," it is crucial that readers consider both illustrations and their accompanying captions and labels as key sources of potentially valuable information.

(cont.)

TABLE 4.1. *(cont.)*

Feature	Discussion of purpose
Diagrams	Diagrams are simplified drawings of a construct or concept described in the text. Their purpose is to help the reader visualize what the author is describing in the running text by illustrating the appearance, structure, or workings of a particular construct or concept.
Charts and graphs	Charts are usually two-dimensional representations of information, and graphs are used to help convey mathematical information. The differences distinguishing diagrams, charts, and graphs from one another are sometimes hard to explain or fathom. Encourage your students to stay focused on what the author's specific purpose is for each feature employed and how that feature helps readers visualize or understand what the author is describing in the running text.
Tables	Tables provide a different way of viewing information presented in the running text. Tables are usually constructed in matrices with rows and columns, and so the reader needs to be aware of how to read the information from top to bottom and left to right, as needed.
Boxes and sidebars	Boxes are boxed-in commentary, highlights, examples (e.g., vignettes, anecdotes, samples), or "asides" related in some way to the running text. Sidebars are usually separate vertical sections of additional text typically set off near the margins of a page. The information in the sidebar may provide additional details supporting the ideas in the running text, or the information may be wholly supplementary and unrelated.
Maps	The maps in texts serve diverse purposes. Most students can readily identify a "map"; the greater difficulty is in identifying the purpose of the map. The map may be a visual depiction of climates in a certain region, or the map may be a representation of the boundaries of states or countries in a region. In one social studies textbook, a map indicated three locations (numbered as 1, 2, 3) where three major events occurred. The events were described briefly with other events in a timeline on the same page and then in more detail in sidebars, each with a number that corresponded to the same number on the map.

ideas presented in the main text. As explained below in Lesson 2, I recommend that students be introduced to multiple features in a short section of text before being asked to deal with them in entire chapters or articles.

■ Lesson 1: Noticing and Learning from Features

Suggestions for Lesson Preparation and Text Study

- **Choose a feature** (like headings) or combination of features (like photographs and captions) to focus on in this lesson; depending on the needs of the students, you may be able to start with a more complex feature or more than one feature. Locate texts with examples of the feature(s) that you will use during a think-aloud at the beginning of the lesson.

- **Study the examples** you have chosen, and plan a think-aloud for at least one. You also need to choose at least one other example for a shared think-aloud with the students. When you plan your own think-aloud, consider what you will say to your students about how one must carefully read the information conveyed in the feature. (See Box 4.1 for an example of a think-aloud.)

- **Create an accessible image** of the sample features you will use during your own think-aloud and the shared think-aloud. Some options include scanning the feature in a book and dropping the image into SMART Board Notebook software, using a document camera to project the original image, or copying the image onto a transparency for use with an overhead projector. If you are meeting with a small group, you can also just use the original text.

  Regardless of how you do this, it is important that students be able to see the feature you are using as an example and that they also be able to see the notes you are writing during your think-aloud.

- **Locate additional texts.** This lesson could occur as part of a content-area unit of study, and you could use a large set of texts on the topic of study during this lesson. I visit the public library and look through numerous books on the topic, checking to see if the books have appropriate features. Then I check out a bunch of these books to use in the lesson. I want the students to have access to at least one book each. I have also used magazines published for children and young adolescents like *National Geographic Explorer* during lessons.

- **Collect materials**, including the following: chart paper, markers, and a few sticky notes for each student.

BOX 4.1. Sample Teacher Think-Aloud about Features and Guided Practice

"READING A FEATURE CLOSELY"

This think-aloud was part of a lesson with a class of students who were studying their state's geography. My objective in this lesson was to have students notice and identify by name two particular features, illustrations and captions, as well as to articulate the purposes of these features while reading content-area trade books. An additional objective was for the students to describe what they learned when they read or examined a feature closely; the engagement described below begins at this point in the lesson. I had planned to discuss two examples with the students, but you'll notice that I followed the lead of the students' enthusiasm and engaged in thinking aloud and guided practice with the same example.

IMPLEMENTING THE THINK-ALOUD

I started by projecting via SMART Notebook an example of a photograph and caption from one of the books the students were perusing (Mattern, 2009, p. 9). The photograph was of two white-tailed deer in the woods, and the caption read: "Illinois's woods are home to a variety of animals, both large and small. These white-tailed deer are among the largest animals in the state and live throughout the area." I demonstrated how to think carefully about the illustration and caption by saying the following as I marked on the SMART Board with one of the pens, circling and underlining as I went:

> When I looked at this picture, I noticed two deer in the woods. [I then circled the images of the deer; next I focused on the caption, reading it aloud.] The words in the caption give me information about the picture and even more information about Illinois. These are not just any deer. These are *white-tailed* deer. [I underlined the words *white-tailed deer.*]

SHARED THINK-ALOUD AND GUIDED PRACTICE

At this point the students were eager to join the think-aloud, so I asked, "What else do you think I might have learned? One student stated enthusiastically, "The white-tailed deer are one of the biggest mammals in Illinois!" When she shared this, I asked, "What words in the caption tell you that?" She read aloud a phrase directly from the caption—"among the largest animals in the state"—and I underlined those words directly on the image on the SMART Board. I also added, "Wow! If I look back at the picture, I can tell these are white-tailed deer because of the white color on their tails." Another student shouted, "And they have white rings around their noses, too!" I marked a circle around both of these details.

When I asked the students to continue thinking about the information in the caption, one of them shared the text, "The woods are home to a variety of animals." I underlined these words and then said, "How can we say that in our own words?" Several children contributed suggestions, and we decided that "different kinds of animals live in the woods in Illinois" might be one way to paraphrase what we had just learned.

Then I engaged the students in shared writing of a sentence describing the knowledge we had developed by paying close attention to the picture and its caption. This is the sentence they composed (as I wrote on the SMART Board):

> I learned that Illinois has woods with many different animals, and these include white-tailed deer.

Suggestions for Implementation of the Lesson

1. **Establish the purpose of the lesson.** These are the language objectives of the lesson that can be posted for students to view and/or stated in student-friendly terms:

   - Notice and identify by name the various features that are found in this informational text.
   - Read or examine each feature closely, and describe in writing and to a peer what you learned from the feature, especially as it relates to the content-area unit of study.

   In addition, you might list specific content-learning objectives and spend a few minutes reviewing the background knowledge that the students have already developed in the content-area unit to date.

2. **Introduce the text, and activate the students' prior knowledge related to features.**

   - *Introduce the set of texts* (books, magazines, etc.) you have chosen, and describe how these texts are related to the content-area unit of study (if that is the case). Hand a text or several texts to each student or group.
   - *Allow the students time to browse* through the texts and enjoy them.
   - *Engage the students in a feature hunt.* Most likely the students are already familiar with the various features that accompany informational text, to some extent. Here is a quick suggestion for helping the students review what they already know about features: for each feature listed below (or that you think is important to include), ask them to hold up their text turned to a page with that particular feature:

o Book or magazine article title	o Diagram
o Chapter title	o Sidebar with additional informa-
o Chapter subtitle	tion
o Photograph with caption	o Bold-faced type
o Map	o Illustration with caption

   A modified introduction may be more appropriate based on the needs of your students. Some options include:

   - o Ask the students to locate a particular feature of your choice.
   - o Write the name of each feature encountered on a piece of chart paper as you go.

    o Share an example of a feature in a text you are holding for them to view before asking the students to seek out that particular feature.

    o Stand near English learners and point carefully to the features, saying the name of each feature aloud clearly and asking individual students to repeat the name of the feature.

3. Explain the importance of paying close attention to each feature found in informational text, and demonstrate this with a teacher think-aloud.

- *Introduce the name of the feature and its purpose.* Explain that an author takes special care to pick just the right features to help him or her explain the topic or ideas in the text.

- *Visually project the example of the feature* for the whole group to view; be prepared to mark on the projected text as you think aloud.

- *Think aloud about the information in the feature.* Mark on the text as you think aloud. (Refer again to Box 4.1 for an example of a teacher think-aloud and guided practice.) Make clear to the students how you determine what is important to notice when examining a feature, and affirm this by marking on the text, underlining, circling, and jotting short notes as you explain what you as a reader do to learn from a feature. Remember to use "I" statements when talking so that students fully appreciate that you, too, are a strategic reader.

- *Engage in modeled writing* of one or two sentences about what you learned about the information imparted by the feature. Remember to think aloud, too, about how you decide to compose the sentences. How did you decide which information to include? You should do this on a piece of chart paper or on a dry erase board for all stduents to view. I like to write these sentences on chart paper or on the SMART Board so that I can use them during the following lesson to review what we did in the first lesson.

4. Engage the students in guided practice with the teacher as coach.

- *Visually project a second example* of the focus feature, and engage the students in a shared think-aloud. Use such prompts as the following:

    What feature did the author decide to use here?

    What do you notice in this feature? What does this feature tell you?

    What are we learning from this feature?

    How did we figure that out?

- *Engage in shared writing* of what was learned (just a few sentences).

5. **Encourage independent practice or practice with a partner, and continue to coach.**

   - *Ask the students to locate the focus feature* in one of the texts they were perusing earlier. They may choose to do this independently or with a partner.
   - *Direct the students to read or examine the feature carefully and write a response,* just as you did earlier together. Hand each student a sticky note to record what he or she learned. (You may decide to give students more than one sticky note if you know they can handle writing about more than one feature during this lesson.)
   - *Confer with individuals or small groups.* You may choose to move around and confer with individual students, or you may prefer to call a small group of students together to work closely with you. Table 4.2 includes descriptions of likely scenarios you may experience during a conference with students while they read and write about features; I have included the language I use when conferring to prompt further thinking. Notice that I am prompting for learning related to being a strategic reader *and* to developing knowledge related to the content-area unit of study.

6. **Close with paired conversations between the students.**

   - *Regroup.*
   - *Ask the students to think–pair–share about what they have written and learned with a peer.* After a few minutes of observing these shared conversations, ask the students to raise their hands if they learned something new about the content area topic. (You do not need to call on students individually to share because you have already observed them by sharing with a peer.)
   - *Close by restating the objectives of the lesson.* For example, you might say:

     > Today we focused on the features of informational text. One particular feature we discussed was (*name the feature studied*). An author will use this feature to (*cite the purpose of the feature*). When you read independently, you need to pay careful attention to this type of feature because this feature will help you understand the ideas in the text better.

7. **Assess and plan your next lesson.**

   - Read your students' sticky notes. What do you notice that you might need to address better in the next lesson? Table 4.3, "Stages of Development in Students' Responses to Features," includes descriptions of what to notice in students' written responses to features and suggestions for follow-up instruction. These suggestions may well apply to more than one developmental

TABLE 4.2. Conferring Scenarios and Suggestions for Coaching

Scenario	Coaching language and actions
The student has not written anything (after being given adequate time to do so).	Prompt: "Tell me a little bit about what you have noticed in this feature."
	If the student does not share anything, say "Why don't we look at this together?" and then move on to reading aloud and thinking aloud about what you learned. You might say, "When I looked at this part of the feature, I noticed . . ." or "I asked myself . . ." or "I thought about what I already knew about . . ."
	If the student does share information, say: "So, I hear you saying that you learned [*revert to what he or she said*], right? Please write that on your sticky note to share with others."
The student has written about the feature—but using a pronoun (e.g., *it*) or a common noun (e.g., *deer*) to refer to the content of the feature or to the feature itself.	Prompt: "When someone else reads your thoughts on this sticky note, what words might you change to make sure they know what you are talking about here?"
The student has copied the text or simply restated what is in the text component of the feature.	Prompt: Gently cover the text and what the student has written. Then ask, "Tell me about what you just learned—*in your own words*."
	Coach the student in using his or her own words, and then state: "When you put this in your own words, this is paraphrasing. When we paraphrase, we usually understand the text better than when we just copy the text."
A student has written a low-quality response, like "This is a map of Illinois."	Prompt: "Tell me more about what you noticed."
	If the student has no response or only responds minimally, say "Let's look at this together."
	After some conversation, say "Share with me what you have learned from this feature now that we have thought about it together."
	Then say, "I think I hear you saying [*repeat what he or she said*], right? Please write that on your sticky note."

level. Keep in mind that students are always at different levels of understanding, depending on what feature is being considered, and they are constantly in the midst of moving from one level of understanding to the next in respect to many features.

- See Table 4.4 (on pages 92–94), "Three Samples of Students' Responses with Teacher Assessment Notes," for examples of student work products, with my notes about what I believe the student is doing well and what he or she needs to focus on learning next.
- Depending on how your students perform during this lesson, you may wish to continue giving similar lessons focused on features not addressed in the

TABLE 4.3. Stages of Development in Students' Responses to Features

Stage of development	Description of the student's responses (oral and written)	Suggestions for follow-up instruction
Attempting	• The student writes or shares aloud information that is not conveyed in the feature, or he or she copies directly from the text. The student may just be resorting to prior knowledge or may actually misunderstand the strategic reading practices being taught.	• Meet one-on-one (3–5 minutes), and as the student shares his or her thinking aloud write notes for the student's later use. This will reduce the cognitive overload the student may be experiencing. • Teach this student in a small group of students with similar needs. As part of a guided reading lesson (15–20 minutes), engage in examining a feature together, thinking aloud about what is being learned, shared writing of what was learned, and conferring with individuals as they practice what you have just done as a small group.
Approaching	• The student is making some sense of the content of the feature(s), but may not yet be synthesizing the key ideas or useful information being imparted. He or she has attempted to write content that is conveyed explicitly in the feature but may be using language he or she has appropriated from the text and does not fully understand or cannot paraphrase properly.	• Before students engage in writing about another feature, share examples of model student entries, or responses. Visually project the examples so that all students can view them, and mark on the examples where the student specifically used words or images that reinforced the lesson's objectives. • Invite students who fall into this category to stay near you—perhaps at a designated table or on the meeting rug—during independent practice so that you can provide additional support more easily.

Meeting	• The student has written content that is explicitly conveyed in the feature and is beginning to include additional meaning that is implicit.
	
	• The student is beginning to make connections to useful prior knowledge related to the content of the feature and to draw valid conclusions about the author's specific use of the feature.
		• Using the lesson framework, introduce a new feature to this student—or the same feature, but with an example that requires even closer reading for the student to fully comprehend the text.
		
		• Engage the student in making a "Features of Nonfiction" handbook with entries that include the following:
		  ○ Purpose of the feature
		  ○ Example of the feature (cut and paste or sketch the feature)
		  ○ Response about what the student learned from the example feature.
		
		• Engage the student in planning to teach younger students about the features found in informational text, using his or her handbook as a model. This might include an initial presentation to a whole class and then partnering with a student to explain the content in the handbook and perhaps to read aloud an informational text with features.

(cont.)

TABLE 4.3. *(cont.)*

Stage of development	Description of the student's responses (oral and written)	Suggestions for follow-up instruction
Exceeding	• The student writes and speaks with ease about the implicit ideas (including how features communicate someone else's perspective) and explicit information conveyed in the feature. • The student is beginning to draw conclusions about the value of using features in nonfiction text, and there has been some transfer of this understanding to work completed at other times during the school day.	• Develop an opportunity for the student to write an expository text, and include appropriate features in that assignment. • Develop an opportunity for the student to add features to an already published text that may not employ features, such as books by author Seymour Simon.

first lesson. However, if your students have a grasp of how to deal with features thoughtfully or are making steady progress in that direction, you may now wish to undertake the second lesson. This instruction focuses on teaching students how to determine what is important and how to synthesize the content of the features with the main text.

■ Lesson 2: Think-Aloud and Guided Practice on Synthesizing Information in the Running Text *and* Features

Prior to the Lesson

I spent 3 days with a group of seventh-grade students studying global warming. Their teacher had noticed that the students were not considering the content of the accompanying features in conjunction with the information in the running text. We decided to undertake the 3-day cycle of lessons described earlier. On the first day, we browsed through library books on global warming and paid close attention to what we could learn from the photographs and captions. On the second day, I wanted the students to think about how the content of the features and the main text combined to convey the author's central ideas. I planned to demonstrate strategic reading of a two-page section of text from the book *Global Warming* (Johnson, 2004) and to model taking notes as I learned. Figure 4.1 (on page 95) shows the specific text I projected for the students to view.

TABLE 4.4. Three Samples of Students' Responses, with Teacher Assessment Notes

Student Response 1

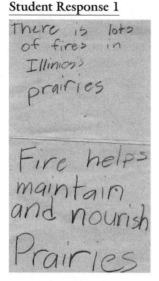

Student's written response.

Fire helps maintain and nourish prairies.

Illustration and caption in *Prairies* (Patent, 1996). Photograph copyright 1996 by William Muñoz. Reprinted by permission.

Assessment Notes for Student Response 1

Attempting: This student has made an assumption that is not stated or conveyed in the combination of features—namely, that there are "lots of fires" (this was not stated in the running text either). It is not unusual for a student to overgeneralize or use language that is not specific. She also copied the caption verbatim as a response.

Follow-up instruction: During a one-on-one conference, use a prompt such as "When you look at this picture/caption, what do you notice?" Wait patiently and then say "Tell me more," if necessary. Once the student begins to share, restate what she has said ("I think I hear you saying that . . .") offering to write this down for her. Finally, review what the student did as a reader, and help her choose the next feature to respond to on her own.

(cont.)

TABLE 4.4. *(cont.)*

Student Response 2

I diden't know
the Asian carpfish
has so many scales
Wow! It swims in the
great lake. It's bright
orange and pearl
white. The carp fish is
beatuful! P. 16

Student's written response.

If the Asian carp ever
entered the Great Lakes,
it would probably become
the dominant fish and
disrupt the food chain.

Illustration and caption in *Illinois* (Burgan, 2008). Photograph 2008 by Peter Arnold.

Assessment Notes for Student Response 2

Approaching stage of development: This student has thought about the photograph carefully, noting the physical characteristics of the carp conveyed in the photo. She has also paid some attention to the information in the caption—naming this fish and noticing that a location, "Great Lake," is named. She has not grasped the main idea in the caption, however. The Asian carp does not yet live in the Great Lakes, and the fish might not seem so appealing if the reader understood that this fish could cause problems for other fish in the Great Lakes.

Follow-up instruction: During a whole-class mini-lesson, think aloud about this sample caption that does more than describe the photo, offering additional information not conveyed in the photo.

Ask this student to sit near you during independent work, and check in with her for a conference whenever needed.

(cont.)

TABLE 4.4. *(cont.)*

Student Response 3

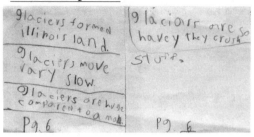

Student's written response.

Thousands of years ago, glaciers similar to this one (above) helped shape the Illinois land. Glaciers can be as much as a mile thick, but usually only move about a foot (30 centimeters) a day.

Photograph and caption in *All Around Illinois: Regions and Resources* (Santella, 2002). Photograph copyright 2002 by Bob and Ira Spring. Reprinted by permission.

Assessment Notes for Student Response 3

Meeting (expectations) stage of development: The student paraphrases information that is stated directly in the caption in his statement "glaciers formed Illinois land." He includes information implied in the caption, writing "glaciers move vary slow" most likely in response to the information stated in the caption "only move about a foot . . . a day." The student includes information that is implied by the picture—"glaciers are huge compared to a man." The student has either activated prior knowledge (we had read an article about the strength of glaciers in a previous lesson) or is using the information in the caption somehow to develop the statement "glaciers are so havey they crush stuff."

Follow-up instruction: Use this student's written response as a model for his peers during a mini-lesson. Affirm what the student is doing well.

Meet with him one-on-one, and begin coaching for reading the running text to see if he learns more than what he derived from the caption and photograph.

Offer a gentle reminder to him and the class as a whole to capitalize letters at the beginning of sentences (as they finish their independent practice and are preparing to share their learning with one another).

FIGURE 4.1. Two-page text from *Global Warming* (Johnson, 2004) visually projected for think-aloud. Reprinted by permission of Hampton-Brown and National Geographic Learning, a part of Cengage Learning. Copyright by National Geographic Learning. Reprinted by permission. All rights reserved.

Implementing the Think-Aloud and Guided Practice

I began the lesson by reviewing the work we had done in the first lesson on examining and understanding features and captions. Then I stated the following:

> When we read informational texts, we need to pay attention to more than just the features in order to determine what is important and how to synthesize the information. What we have to do is think about how the information in the features and the main text *work together* to help us understand the author's central ideas.

Next, I shared a cake baking analogy to help the students better understand. I asked them to list ingredients for a cake, and as they did I drew a rough sketch of each listed ingredient on the board and put a plus sign between each ingredient. I finished the equation by drawing an equal sign at the end of the list and then sketched the completed cake. I said:

What we have to do to read strategically is think about all of the ingredients or elements the author has included, like the headings and subheadings, the captions and photographs, and the main text. As we think about the ingredients, we can begin to determine the author's central idea. When we do that, it's like stirring together and baking the ingredients for a cake. The finished cake then represents our understanding of the author's central idea. Let me show you what I mean.

I then projected the image of the text on global warming. I started my think-aloud by drawing separate circles around the heading "How Well Are We Doing?" and the subheadings "Good News" and "Bad News." I read these aloud as I drew the circles and then thought aloud by saying the following:

Well, I know this book is about global warming. So, I'm thinking the author is going to tell me about what we know is happening. Because he has written "good news" and "bad news," I'm thinking there must be some positive effects of global warming as well as negative effects. I have never thought of there being positive effects, so I definitely want to read more.

At this point, the students were eager to contribute, so I followed their lead and we engaged in a shared think-aloud—with me stepping in and stepping back as needed. I started by saying, "If I am going to take in all of the information on these two pages, what do I need to do now?" One of the students responded, "Read the captions and look at the pictures." As we read and discussed each of these features, I drew arrows directed at the feature. Doing this helps the students keep track of what we are discussing and how we are being strategic. Through our conversation the students revealed to themselves how one picture and caption showed a positive effect of global warming—two people in Colorado farming during a longer growing season—and the other picture and caption showed a negative effect—sea lions possibly having to struggle to survive in Alaska if there are warmer temperatures.

When we started to read the two columns of bulleted text, I stepped in and thought aloud by saying the following:

When I look at these lists, I am thinking there is a lot of information.

While I was not expecting the students to determine what was important specifically in this lesson, I did want to model this careful reading for them. I continued by saying:

> So as I read each bullet, I am going to think carefully about what content I want to remember.

I read aloud the text by the first bullet:

> Global warming may lead to shorter, warmer winters.

And then I said:

> I already know I'm reading about global warming. What I want to remember is the effects of global warming. I'm going to underline the phrase "shorter, warmer winters" to help me remember this particular effect.

We continued by engaging in a shared think-aloud about the rest of the bulleted points under "Good News."

Scaffolding for Independent Practice

I wanted the students to try reading strategically on their own, but I wanted to make sure they understood the steps they needed to take. So, I asked the students to share aloud with me what we had just done as strategic readers to "tackle" the text. On a piece of chart paper, I wrote as we generated a list of steps for strategic reading:

- Read the title and subheadings. Make a prediction about what I will be reading.
- Read the pictures and captions, and take notes about what I learned.
- Read the text and think about what is important to remember. Take notes.
- Compare what I learned in the text to what I learned in the features, and write about what I think is the author's central idea.

Then I asked the students to strategically read this same two-page section of text again, but on their own. They read and jotted down notes. In the example in Figure 4.2, you can see how the student placed the sticky notes (as I directed the students to) in a way intended to convey what she understood about strategic reading. Her notes include identification of the central idea in the main text and two supporting examples and a summary of the content in each of the pictures and captions. Her final note, written inside a drawn image of a decorated cake, states the author's central idea.

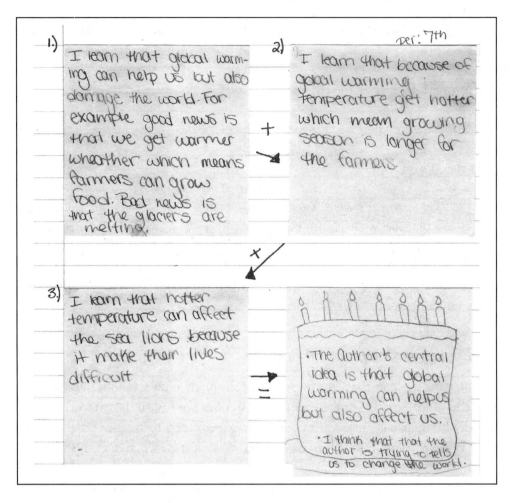

FIGURE 4.2. Example of a student's notes.

Follow-Up Lesson for More Practice

On the following day, I met with these students again for a third lesson. I projected examples of their responses from the second lesson, and together we identified what the students had done well. Then I asked the students to write their own strategic plans for reading on a large sticky note. See Figure 4.3 for an example of one student's plan. Figure 4.4 presents a photograph of how one student used his notes from close reading to write an extended response.

I followed by asking them to tackle another two-page section in the same book on global warming. As in the previous lesson, they took their notes on sticky notes. As the students finished, I met with individuals or small groups and

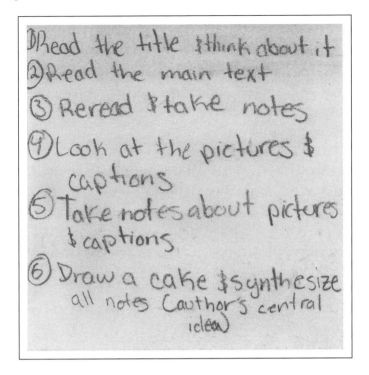

FIGURE 4.3. Example of a student's strategic reading plan.

FIGURE 4.4. A student using his notes from close reading to write a response.

asked them to write a longer response using their notes. I made clear the steps in this process (which I had posted on a piece of chart paper at the front of the room) and then asked them to "give it a try."

If your students have been writing in response to texts you have read aloud or that they have read independently, they should move into this task fairly easily. This particular group of seventh graders was not familiar with writing in response to informational texts. To scaffold the process of moving from taking notes to writing responses, I posted clearly written directions for completing this task on the front board. Depending on the needs of your students, you might have to wait until the next lesson to proceed further. In a follow-up lesson, you might consider projecting the image of one student's notes and then engage the group in shared writing of a response, using that particular student's notes as a common reference point.

▪ What's Next?

As a result of these lessons, your students may be ready to attempt strategic reading of longer texts. As will be seen in Chapter 5, the next instructional task is to teach the students how to use what they know about synthesis as well as what they know about how texts are developed (with diverse features that support and extend the main text) to preview a text strategically and to set forth a shared purpose for reading.

CHAPTER FIVE

Strategic Previewing of a Text to Set a Purpose

Typically, students beginning to read an informational text just open to the first page and immediately start to read. Instead, they need to slow down and take the time to *preview the text strategically*. This approach includes not only paying attention to the accompanying features that they have learned about in earlier instruction but also stopping to think about how these features provide readers with clues about the information they will be encountering. After previewing the text properly and predicting what the author will address, the student can then set a clear purpose for reading.

The results of teaching students to preview a text strategically can be amazing—particularly in the area of identity and agency of the reader. A fourth grader once bragged to his teacher, "I feel like I already know what the whole chapter is about!" This chapter focuses on teaching students to preview texts strategically, particularly by using an instructional mnemonic known as THIEVES. Table 5.4 at the end of the chapter (page 116) includes additional mnemonics that can be used for previewing a text. The instructional practices described for introducing and using THIEVES can be applied to any of these mnemonics as well.

■ Consider Your Students' Strengths and Needs

What have your observations or formative assessments revealed about how your students preview a text and set their purpose for reading?

- Do they typically begin reading the running text without studying or even considering the various accompanying features in the text?
- Do they simply page through the text, but in a casual way without any clear purpose?
- Do they make predictions that are not informed by having previewed the text—predictions that might lead the reader astray?
- Do their predictions reveal careful thinking about the information gathered prior to reading as well as their own background knowledge?

Students need to be able to make a relevant and coherent prediction and then use this prediction to set a meaningful purpose for reading. Previewing the text and setting a purpose for reading—without being prompted by the teacher—is a reading habit that prepares the student to understand the text at a deeper level.

■ Where to Start? Teaching the THIEVES Mnemonic

The primary lesson described in this chapter focuses on introducing THIEVES, a strategic approach to previewing text in depth (adapted from Manz, 2002). THIEVES was developed as a way of helping students activate their background knowledge and make predictions about the content they will be encountering while reading. Consider the metaphor of a thief. When you take something that is not yours, what are you trying to do? You are trying to get ahead! If we preview a text, in a sense we are trying to get ahead of the author. We are trying to get on top of the content by being able to predict some of the author's central ideas and then by comparing these predictions to what we already know about these ideas. THIEVES is a playful mnemonic that can be used to focus students' attention on the importance of previewing a text before starting to read.

The letters in the word *thieves* form an acronym that reminds readers of the specific features in the text that they should study prior to a closer reading (Manz, 2002). Table 5.1 identifies the features named in the acronym and the questions a reader might naturally ask in considering these features. The key point is to try to identify the central idea(s) of the text as one moves through each step, gathering more and more information to make informed predictions. Also, after students preview the features and other elements of the text (e.g., "every first sentence") named in the mnemonic THIEVES, they need to pause and summarize what they think the text will be all about, based on their strategic preview.

TABLE 5.1. The THIEVES Mnemonic

Feature or element of the text to be previewed	Questions the reader might ask when considering the named feature or element of the text
T—Title	What does the title make me think the text will be about? What might be the central message the author is trying to communicate? What do I already know about this subject?
H—Headings	How has the author divided the content of this text into smaller topics? What are these smaller topics? Based on these topics, what do I think I will read about in each section? How does that relate to the larger ideas in the text?
I—Introduction	What does the introduction do to make me curious about this subject?
E—Every first sentence in each section	What additional details can I gather about the content of the text?
V—Visuals and Vocabulary	What do the accompanying features like figures, captions, and boxed information tell me about the content of this article? Are there words in boldface type or italics that I need to pay special attention to as I preview the text? What do they mean?
E—End-of-article or end-of-chapter questions	How does the author wrap up the writing? What questions will I be asked to answer?
S—Summarize thinking	If I think about all of the information I have gathered, what do I predict I will be reading about? What do I think the author's central ideas will be in this text?

■ Focus Lesson: Introducing Strategic Previewing of Text with THIEVES

This lesson introduces students to the concept of "getting ahead" by strategically previewing the text and its features and making predictions about their content and the author's key ideas.

Suggestions for Lesson Preparation and Text Study

- **Locate copies of an appropriate instructional level text.** If you are working with a whole class, locate a sufficient number of texts that students will be able to read with only minimal scaffolding. In the past, I have created text sets (so, not all the texts are the same, but they all focus on the same content-area unit of study) for this lesson, or else I have located the same text written at different instructional levels. If you are working with a small group, choose a text all the students can read with only minimal direct support from you.

- **Create a visually accessible image** of part of the chosen text—most likely a two-page spread—that you can use in thinking aloud in front of the students. I usually choose the first part of a core text that everyone in the group will be reading or a text segment from the set of texts I have compiled.

- **Prepare your think-aloud.** Plan for what you will say to demonstrate how you preview the text and features strategically and, as a result, how you predict what the article will be about (see Box 5.1).

- **Create THIEVES bookmarks**. Make a copy of the THIEVES bookmark for each student to use during guided and independent reading practice. Figure 5.1 shows a sample bookmark I have used with students. Modify the bookmark, based on the needs of your students. For example, I have experimented with making the second *E* stand for the "end of an article," or the conclusion. I ask students to write their predictions and thoughts on lined paper as they preview the text; you might ask them to write the mnemonic down the left-hand side of a blank sheet of paper and then take notes as they preview the text. Also make a visually accessible image of the THIEVES bookmark; you will need to be able to write on this image during the think-aloud (see Figure 5.2).

T – Title
H – Headings
I – Introduction
E – Every 1st sentence
V – Visuals & Vocabulary
E – End of chapter questions
S – Summary

FIGURE 5.1. THIEVES bookmark.

BOX 5.1. Suggestions for Demonstrating Previewing and Predicting with Feature-Packed Texts

I remember I had been talking with educators in the field about using the THIEVES mnemonic as an activity for teaching students to preview and predict for a while, but I had never actually taught the lessons I was suggesting. A small group of fourth-grade teachers invited me to come to their school and "walk the talk," and I jumped at the chance. I immediately started planning, using a severe-weather science text the fourth graders were reading, and then—oh, my—did I stumble! I soon realized there were just too many features in each chapter for students to manage. As a result I modified my thinking drastically, and created instead a lesson plan to use the THIEVES mnemonic with two-page spreads of text only. These two pages typically included a title, deck, two figures with captions, and a map as well as the main text. My goal for the students became to think through THIEVES for each of four two-page spreads and then write a summary sentence after each. Looking at all four summary sentences, then, the students could make a prediction about the whole chapter.

PREPARING AND IMPLEMENTING THE THINK-ALOUD

The notes I wrote in preparation are shown in the figure below.

I walked myself through how a reader might preview the two pages of text on "droughts." I not only thought about my predictions but also how these tied into the author's central idea for this two-page spread. Going through this process for myself helped me articulate for the students during the think-aloud. For the lesson, I made transparencies of the two pages of text and the THIEVES bookmark. In advance, I even drew my own picture of a thief (my little brother sneaking away with my Halloween candy—see Figure 5.2).

During the lesson, I switched between the transparency of the THIEVES bookmark and transparencies of the text. I used the THIEVES bookmark as a way to keep track of my previewing and checked off each letter in the acronym as I previewed the text. I also marked on the transparencies of the text as I thought aloud about each feature named in the THIEVES mnemonic. So, for example, when I read the title, I circled it. Seeing me mark on the text as the students hear me think aloud serves as a visual support for the process I am modeling. At a certain point the students wanted to join in on the think-aloud. We finished by composing a summary sentence of what we thought the text would be about and also setting a purpose for reading.

Then we read the text (each student read silently) and regrouped. The students were amazed at how much they had learned even before they read. I moved into guided practice by asking the students to try out the THIEVES mnemonic with another two-page section of this text. As they read, they took notes on a blank sheet of paper, and I walked around to confer with individual students. As each child finished one section of text, I asked him or her to use the mnemonic to preview the next two-page section of text and predict and read until they were done.

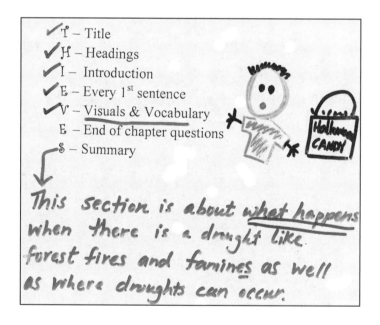

FIGURE 5.2. The notes I took in front of the students as I did the think-aloud.

Suggestions for Implementation of the Lesson

1. **Establish the purposes of the lesson.** These are the language objectives of the lesson, which can be posted for students to view and/or stated aloud in student-friendly terms:
   - Preview the text strategically while using the mnemonic THIEVES.
   - Make an informed prediction about the author's central idea before reading the text closely.

2. **Introduce the text, and activate the students' background knowledge about the topic.** Hopefully, this text is part of a content-area unit of study, and you can easily activate background knowledge on the topic or subject of the text. One suggestion is to ask students to browse through the text and talk to their partner about what they think the text will be about. This is an informal approach to previewing the text, and you can later compare and contrast this experience with the strategic previewing you will be introducing next.

3. **Explain the necessity of systematically previewing a text to make thoughtful predictions, introduce the THIEVES strategy, and then demonstrate it while engaged in a teacher think-aloud.**
   - *Explain the skills involved in previewing and predicting before reading.* Many of your students may be familiar with these concepts already, but they also may take these skills for granted and not implement them. You might start by asking:

     When you read an informational article, do you ever just begin reading at the first paragraph? Or maybe you casually look through the article, but you are doing this mainly to see if it will be interesting?

   Many of your students will nod in response.
   You might continue by saying:

     When you want to really understand an informational text, you need to start by *previewing* the text. When you preview the text, you are in a sense getting ahead of the author. You are getting a sense of what the article is going to be about and starting to think about what you already know about some of the ideas that are in the article. When you pause after previewing and think about all of the information you have gathered, you can make thoughtful predictions about what the article is going to be about. This will prepare you for reading the actual text. You can think about what the author is trying to say in this text and set a purpose for reading. You might be surprised how much you already know about the text as you read—because you previewed strategically, predicted thoughtfully, and set a clear purpose as a result.

- *Introduce the THIEVES mnemonic.* Tell the students you are going to share an activity that will help them practice previewing the text strategically and then make thoughtful predictions. Hand the sticky notes out, and ask the students to draw a picture of what they think about when they visualize the word *thief*. Give the students 2–3 minutes to sketch, and then ask them to share with their peers nearby. If needed, share your own sketch of a thief. Then pose this question to the students: "What is the purpose of being a thief?" The students replying may mention stealing, getting something you want, or the like. I don't wish to focus unduly on "thievery" or "stealing," so I offer an alternative way of thinking about that subject by saying the following:

  > A thief is trying to get ahead. He or she feels that if one takes something in particular one will be better off.

  You might briefly discuss how this description of a thief's purpose applies to the students' sketched versions of thieves.
      Then you might say:

  > We can be "thieves" when we read a new text in that we can get ahead and feel like we know more about what we will be reading!

  Place a copy of the THIEVES bookmark with its key words or phrases on the overhead projector or document camera for students to view, and pass out the bookmarks for students to place their sticky notes on. (See Figure 5.3 for an example of one student's sketch and bookmark.) Continue by saying:

  > When we preview a text, we need to look at particular features and elements of the text.

  List aloud the different features and elements in THIEVES. Continue by saying:

  > By thinking carefully about each one of these, we can start thinking about what we already know about the topic and the facts that the author might be including in the text. Let me show you how I do this as a reader.

- *Project the sample text, and then think aloud about it.* Using the notes you prepared, think aloud about the article or section title in the sample text. I use

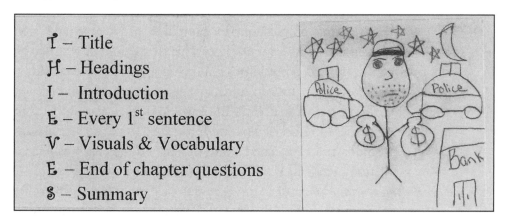

T – Title
H – Headings
I – Introduction
E – Every 1st sentence
V – Visuals & Vocabulary
E – End of chapter questions
S – Summary

FIGURE 5.3. Example of the THIEVES bookmark and a student's sketch of a thief.

a marker to draw lines under the title or to put an asterisk next to the title so that the students will understand exactly which feature I am thinking aloud about as I preview. I also remove the text and replace it with the THIEVES bookmark from time to time. I write notes on the bookmark as I go or check off that I have previewed the features or text named in the acronym.

4. **Engage the students in guided practice, acting as their coach.**
   - *Continue by next collaboratively* previewing the text, using the THIEVES mnemonic. At this point, your students should be eager to join you. Ask them to preview the next feature in the THIEVES mnemonic, and then solicit their oral responses.
   - *Engage in the shared writing of notes.* After a shared think-aloud, the students may be ready to try this out on their own. Start by asking them to preview independently the next feature in the THIEVES mnemonic, and then regroup as a whole class to discuss what they were thinking. As particular students are called on to share their thoughts, you might jot down their predictions or thoughts for the whole group to view on the visually projected THIEVES bookmark. When I do this, I put the student's initials next to his or her comment. This reinforces the sense of collaboration.

5. **Encourage the students' who practice *independently* and continue to confer with them.**
   - *Ask the students to "try out" THIEVES.* When your observations of the students lead you to believe they are ready to work on their own, ask the students to finish previewing the text by following the steps in THIEVES.

Once they finish taking notes about their predictions, they should look through their notes and write a summary of what they think the text will be about or what the author's central ideas will be. As noted previously, this is typically the point when many students may appear confused or indecisive. If this is their first lesson with THIEVES, I would then engage students in shared writing of the summary of what was previewed. After they have written their predictions and have stated a purpose for reading that was related to those predictions, students should read the text independently.

- *Confer during continued practice.* As in previous chapters, I have listed some common scenarios that might develop and the language teachers can use to move students forward (see Table 5.2).

6. Close with conversation—the synthesis of content and reflection on strategic reading having been accomplished.

- *Regroup.*
- *Ask students to engage in a 10-minute quick write.* Post the following two questions for the students to answer: What did you learn when you read this

TABLE 5.2. Common Conferring Scenarios and Suggestions for Coaching

Scenario	Coaching language and actions
The student is off-task.	Prompt: "Tell me what you are doing to preview the text." If needed, follow with "So, what do you need to do next?"
The student has looked at a feature or element in the text but has not been able to write notes yet.	Prompt: "When you looked at that feature or part of the text, what did you predict the text would be about?" and then "Why do you think so?"
	If needed, offer to write the first note for the student as he or she responds orally.
	Summarize aloud what you heard the student say, and then ask him or her to repeat it. Encourage him or her to immediately write down what he or she just said.
The student has written notes easily, but only about features that are easily understood.	Possible prompts: • "When you looked at this diagram (or photograph or chart, etc.), what were you thinking in your mind?" • "How did this help you understand the text better?"
The student is writing notes easily and may need a push to think more deeply about his or her predictions, perhaps by activating background knowledge.	Possible prompts: • "What does this make you think about that you already know? Why?" • "How does thinking about what you already know strengthen your prediction?"

text? How did previewing the text help you as a reader? Ask the students to write their response. If you have time, you can ask the students to share their responses in groups of three or four. If you do not have time for the quick write, you can use this task as a way to warm up during the following lesson.

- *Close by reviewing the goals of the lesson* and restating the importance of previewing a text systematically and making thoughtful predictions about not only the content of the text but also the author's central ideas.

7. Assess and plan your next lesson.

- Read the students' written response, determine what you need to teach next, and choose some supportive examples to share in a follow-up lesson. See suggestions for follow-up instruction in Table 5.3.
- Table 5.3 includes descriptions of students' stages of development in previewing and predicting that I have observed. Use this as a tool for getting a general grasp of the kinds of predictions your students are making, based on their analysis of the text's features, such as the first sentence after each section heading.
- The examples of student responses shared in Table 5.3 are from a group of fifth-grade students who read an article titled "Thirsty Planet" (Geiger, 2010). The author's central idea is that water is a finite resource that every living creature, whether animal or plant, needs access to in order to survive.

TABLE 5.3. Stages of Development in Previewing and Predicting

Description of student's responses (oral or written)	Suggestions for follow-up instruction
Attempting stage	
• The student writes or states aloud predictions that are *not* based on evidence in the text; the student may be drawing too heavily from background knowledge. *Example from the student's notes:* Pollution is overruling the planet so bad, people can't even drink clean water. *Explanation:* The student wrote this prediction after looking at the title, deck, and photograph; there is no indication from the evidence in these features that the author will be discussing the issue of pollution.	• Implement a mini-lesson that includes a teacher think-aloud in which one models making relevant predictions with evidence in the text to support these predictions and also models making predictions that are not supported in the text.

(cont.)

TABLE 5.3. *(cont.)*

Description of student's responses (oral or written)	Suggestions for follow-up instruction

Attempting stage *(cont.)*

• The student veers away from writing about the content of the text to writing about the purpose of the feature or text referred to in the mnemonic. *Example from the student's notes:* They tell me what the story is going to be like or what it's about. *Explanation:* The student wrote this in his or her notes next to the first *E* in the mnemonic THIEVES for "every first sentence." He or she has made a prediction about what every first sentence will tell him or her. Instead, he or she needs to read the first sentence of each section of the text and predict the content of the text.	• Meet with a small group and engage in a shared think-aloud as the group collaborates to preview a text by using the THIEVES mnemonic. Engage the group members in the shared writing of notes about their predictions.

Approaching stage

• The student writes or states aloud predictions that either restate the text or are very literal interpretations. *Example from student's notes:* This will be about the wonders of water. *Explanation:* The student has simply restated the subheading "The Wonder of Water." The student may not be interpreting what the author means by "wonder of water" and therefore may not be making a real prediction. • The student's predictions are listed as though he or she is mindlessly filling in a blank. *Example from the student's notes:* This will be about how there is a lot of water on the Earth, how water has been around for millions of years, how every plant and animal needs water, and how people need water, too. *Explanation:* It is clear that the student has previewed the text, because all of these ideas are addressed in the article. This response lacks depth; there is no indication from the student about the author's central idea and the reason the author might be putting all of these details into one text.	• During a mini-lesson, share examples of students' THIEVES notes that reveal an interpretation of particular features (see examples of the student's notes in "meeting stage" below). • During a mini-lesson, write aloud in front of the students. Write a prediction that lists several ideas. Engage the students in conversation about what this prediction reveals and what is missing. Engage in the shared writing of an additional sentence that elaborates further. For example, an additional sentence for the example shared (at left) might be the following: I'm thinking the author wants to share how water plays a major role in life on Earth.

Meeting stage

• The student writes or states aloud responses tying the information gathered during the preview to a prediction about the author's central ideas. *Written example from a student's notes after reading every first sentence:* Reading every first sentence made me think it's about different creatures trying to survive with little water.	• With a group of students who are meeting expectations, engage them in a conversation about how to effectively move away from the use of the THIEVES bookmark to preview the text independently.

(cont.)

TABLE 5.3. *(cont.)*

Description of student's responses (oral or written)	Suggestions for follow-up instruction
Meeting stage *(cont.)*	
Explanation: If you read the first two to three sentences in each section of the article, you could make this prediction. The student has synthesized the information and written a prediction about one of the author's central ideas.	• Ask this group to keep a log throughout the day (for just a few days) with notes about when they independently previewed texts systematically and how this was helpful.
• The student's summary of what he or she predicts the text will be about reveals synthesis of the information gathered. *Written example from the student's notes:* I think that it will be about how people and animals need water, how they struggle for it, and what they use it for. *Explanation:* The student has identified three central ideas in the text.	
• The student identifies evidence in the text to support his or her predictions. *Written example from the student's notes:* I think this article is going to be about how hard it is to get water because there is a picture with a caption about people in Kenya walking really far to get their water and another picture of two girls sweeping mud from a watering trough. There's also a picture of Salton City, California, that looks like a desert and the people have to have their water pumped to them.	
• The student is beginning to rely on his or her own sense of agency when previewing and predicting; he or she is not limiting him- or herself to a lockstep application of the THIEVES steps.	
Exceeding stage	
• Without the aid of the THIEVES bookmark, the student previews the text fluently, sharing aloud what he or she is thinking and making references to information in the text that supports his or her predictions. The student's predictions are relevant and reveal a synthesis of the content gathered during the preview.	• As needed, review previewing the text.

■ Follow-Up Lesson

When I assessed the THIEVES notes written by the group of fifth graders who read the magazine article "Thirsty Planet" (Geiger, 2010), I noticed that the students' notes were very list-like. The students did not always think *across* the content revealed in the headings, or in every first sentence, or in all of the visuals to make their predictions. As a result, I planned a mini-lesson to model this skill. I used the same article from the first lesson and demonstrated reading and thinking about the information conveyed in each first sentence in each section. For example, these are the first (and occasionally second) sentences in each section.

- Water covers 70 percent of Earth's surface.
- Water has been recycled like this for millions of years.
- Where there's water, animals can't be far behind.
- Animals don't just crawl, walk, slither, or fly to water. Many live in it.
- You need water, too.
- With so many demands on our fresh water supply, do we have enough?
- To solve some of these problems, people are getting creative.

Using a document camera, I turned to each page as I read aloud the first sentences and made the text accessible for viewing. The students each had a copy of the article as well. After I read aloud the sentences, I thought aloud.

> As I was reading these sentences and sometimes rereading them, I began to think that this article is about how water is a precious resource. There's a lot of water because it covers 70% of the Earth's surface, but I know we can't use it all because a lot of it is salt water. Also, there's not an infinite amount of water—I want to know more about this, for sure. It seems like if we are recycling water, then there is a limited amount. Yet animals need water, and we need water, and I know plants need water. I know what I do to save water, but I'm curious to see what the author shares. So, again, I think I'm going to be reading about how every living thing needs water, but there's only so much of it, and we have to figure out how to share and conserve water.

As I thought aloud, I returned to different first sentences in the text and underlined key words that were part of my think-aloud. For example, I underlined "70 percent of Earth's surface" as I spoke. It is important to debrief with students about what you demonstrated before setting them off to give this a try. So, I posed the questions, "What did I just do to preview the text?" and "How did that help me start to think about the author's central ideas?"

Then I asked the students to meet in groups to engage in using THIEVES. Students can get tired of this approach to previewing a text if you ask them to write notes every time they use the mnemonic. I wanted them to see THIEVES as a tool they could use flexibly, with the end goal of a thoughtful prediction related to the author's central idea. So, for this lesson, I asked the students to preview the text aloud in small groups (see Figure 5.4). As a group, they would be collectively accountable for previewing strategically and then talking to one another about what they had noticed about similar features—in a way that was like the process I modeled with every first sentence.

After the students previewed and predicted what they would be reading as it related to the author's central idea, they each read the article silently and then got

FIGURE 5.4. Students meeting in circles to preview and make predictions about an article. Notice the rectangular THIEVES bookmarks scattered around the meeting space.

back together with their groups to talk about what they had learned. This particular class of students had been meeting in literature circles for several weeks. So they understood how to summarize what they read and then continue to share. If your students have not previously met in literature circles or any kind of discussion group, you would need to instruct them in how to have a meaningful conversation before undertaking this lesson.

■ What's Next?

Students will be further ahead as readers if they preview and then predict the text. Using their predictions, they can more easily identify the author's central ideas as they read. The trick is then to read the text with a sustained purpose focused on determining what is important and synthesizing. This requires self-monitoring or thinking about one's thinking while reading. The next chapter explains self-monitoring in more detail and includes suggestions for helping students become more efficient in using this strategy.

TABLE 5.4. Additional Mnemonics for Previewing Informational Texts

TELL—Conceptually, previewing the text helps us tell ourselves or someone else our predictions for the topic and central idea of the text.

Title	• What does the title tell us about the topic or central idea of the text?
Examine	• Examine the text features. What clues do the features provide about the topic or central idea of the text?
Look	• Look *at* **bold** words or words in *italics*. Use these words to make a prediction about the topic or central idea of the text.
Look	• Look *up* and predict what the text will be about overall—based on your preview of the text in the first three steps of TELL.

HIP—Conceptually, it is "hip" to be a reader.

Headings	• Read and think about the information provided in the headings.
Introduction	• Read and think about the information provided in the introduction.
Prediction	• Make a prediction about the topic or central idea of the text.

CATAPULT—Conceptually, when we preview a text, we are catapulting ourselves forward in understanding the text. Share a visual of someone being catapulted and then the mnemonic. This mnemonic might be best used with a narrative text that describes an endeavor, journey, or the work of a particular group.

Covers	• What do you notice when you look at the cover of a text? What does this make you think the book will be about?
Author	• What does the author's page say at the end of the text about his or her expertise on this topic? Or the research they completed to write about this topic?
Title	• What does the title of the text tell you about the topic? And possibly the author's central idea?
Audience	• Who was the text written for? Why do you think the author would want this audience to know about this topic or central idea?
Page 1	• Read page 1 and make a prediction about the topic and the author's central idea.
Underlying message	• Think about what you have already previewed. What do you think the author's central idea is going to be? Why? What's your evidence?
Look at features	• What do the text features like photos, diagrams, and maps tell us?
Time, place, important people	• From what you have previewed so far, what can you say about when the topic of this article takes place? Where this event takes place? The important people described? What do you think the people will be doing? Or learning?

Note. TELL is adapted from variations of the mnemonic TELLS available on the Internet. HIP was created by my colleague Jamie Heraver, a reading specialist who works closely with intermediate-grade English learners. CATAPULT is adapted from Zwiers (2004). Copyright 2004 by the International Reading Association. Adapted by permission.

CHAPTER SIX

Self-Monitoring While Reading Informational Texts

Many times when a student is reading an informational text, his or her mind begins to wander to other matters or the meaning of the text begins to break down and yet the student continues to read without fully comprehending the text. When the teacher confers with a student in this predicament, he or she might say, "Tell me about what you have been reading," and the student will typically respond, "I have no idea!"

One of the wonderful things about working with children and young adolescents is that they can be blatantly honest sometimes. When introducing the concept of "self-monitoring," I always start by asking the students: "Does your mind ever wander while you're reading? Do you think about what you're going to be eating for lunch, instead? Or about what you're going to be doing after school?" Without fail, they answer with a resounding "Yes!"

Think about when you are driving home and your mind wanders to the problems of the day. Do you ever wonder how you got home? Similarly, our minds can wander when we are reading, and this happens frequently to our students.

■ Consider Your Students' Strengths and Needs

What have your observations or formative assessments revealed about your students' effective self-monitoring while reading informational text? What have you noticed that makes you think your students might need to work on self-monitoring?

- When students confer with you:
  - Do they recall only the last fact they read in the text?
  - Do they have to look back at the text to remember what they read?
  - Do they cite ideas directly from the text instead of paraphrasing in their own words?
- When students write about what they have read:
  - Do they write about the content from only the end of a text they have read?
  - Do they name only the topic and provide no details about or elaboration of the content they have read?
  - Do they write about what they knew about the topic before reading instead of what they learned while reading?

When we teach for self-monitoring, we are impressing on the critical importance of staying focused on understanding the text (i.e., learning and critiquing the content the author is sharing). The student as a reader needs to develop and use a repertoire of strategies such as asking questions and determining importance flexibly. He or she also needs to be aware of when meaning is beginning to break down and immediately employ fix-up strategies to make better sense of the text. If the student can self-monitor his or her reading successfully, he or she is on the path to deeper understanding of the author's central ideas.

■ Where to Start? Teaching the Coding Method

Two lessons are described in this chapter. The first lesson introduces students to self-monitoring through an activity called the coding method (Hoyt, 2008). The second lesson is a sample follow-up lesson I gave to a group of students after assessing their written responses in the first lesson.

The coding method (Hoyt, 2008) is an activity that encourages students to focus on *thinking about their own thinking*. The student is told to consider the following questions (or possible reactions) as he or she reads:

- "Is this new information for me?"
- "Is this information I *already knew*? (e.g., What do I already know from the content-area unit we are studying in class?)"
- "What do I *not understand* about this information? Or, what are my questions?"
- "Wow, this is really cool stuff!"

The following codes can be projected onto a screen or copied onto bookmarks for students to consider. Students can then use these codes to label their thinking—mentally and in writing.

+   This is new information.
*   I already knew this information.
?   I wonder . . . or I don't understand . . .
!   Wow!

When I first started teaching the coding method, the students wrote just the single-character code for their thinking on a 3″×3″ sticky note that they placed in the text; but, when I conferred with them later, they couldn't recall what they were thinking when they originally notated that particular passage. Now, I encourage students to stop at the end of a section of text, write the code notation onto a sticky note or piece of paper, and then jot down a few thoughts so that later they can remember what they were thinking.

The trick with teaching the students to properly use the codes is to emphasize the importance of using them not only to help them think about their thinking but also to begin to ponder the author's central idea(s), that is, to synthesize the text. Students *love* coding, but this can become a mindless fill-in-the-blank activity; a student might post dozens of sticky notes on pages and then, after all that work, still end up with only a shallow understanding of the text. From the beginning, we need to make clear that as students code they need to think about how their thinking relates to the key ideas in the text—in other words, they need to *code mindfully*.

The lessons described below are a great opportunity to use texts related to a content-area unit of study. The students can tap background knowledge they have already developed during the unit of study while also building up new knowledge. If you choose a text on a totally unfamiliar subject, however, some background-knowledge building needs to be undertaken with students prior to the lesson.

■ Lesson 1: Self-Monitoring Using the Coding Method

Suggestions for Lesson Preparation and Text Study

- **Locate copies of an instructional-level text.** If you are working with a whole class, locate a sufficient number of texts that students will be able to read with only nominal teacher support. In the past, I have created my own text sets (in which not all the texts are identical, but they all focus on the same content-area unit of study) for this lesson, or I have located the same text written at different instructional levels. Several publishers have begun to make the same text written at different text complexities available. For example, National Geographic provides the magazine *National Geographic Explorer* written at a "pioneer" level (2nd–3rd grade) and at a "pathfinder" level (4th–5th grade). If you are working with a small group, choose a text written at the students' instructional level (i.e., they can read the text with scaffolding support from you that is gradually diminished).

- **Create a visually accessible image** of the portion of the text that you will be thinking aloud about in front of the students. I usually choose the first part of the core text that all group members will be reading or a text from the set I have specially compiled.

- **Study the text and prepare your think-aloud.** Choose a section of text that you will read aloud to the students, and then share how you self-monitored your reading by using one of the code notations. Consider the needs of your students. Do you want to introduce fewer codes at the beginning? Do you need to model codes that students may be reluctant to try, such as "I don't understand"? Write notes that you can place next to the specific text citation for students to view as you think aloud (see Figure 6.1). You might also plan to

---

DEMONSTRATING SELF-MONITORING WITH USE OF THE CODING METHOD.
(5 minutes)

This whole group lesson was part of an earth science unit on land formations. The article is about the eruption of volcano Eyja in Iceland (Ruane, 2010). The author begins the article with a description of one family quickly evacuating their home after receiving a call that Eyja, a short distance from their home, was erupting.

   This think-aloud started 5 minutes into the lesson after the students and I discussed the title, deck, and introduction. During this initial conversation, we predicted that the topic of the article would be about what it is like to live near a volcano when it erupts; as a result, we were beginning to think about the author's central idea for the article. I followed by introducing the concept of self-monitoring and the coding method. Then I placed the page in Figure 1 minus my notes on the document camera for everyone to view. As you read through what I said during the think-aloud (in clockwise order), notice how I demonstrate self-monitoring for not only what I am thinking about that particular chunk of text, but also for how it relates to the bigger ideas in the text.

(cont.)

FIGURE 6.1. Sample teacher think-aloud. Text reprinted by permission of Hampton-Brown and National Geographic Learning, a part of Cengage Learning. Copyright by National Geographic Learning. Reprinted by permission. All rights reserved. Photograph reprinted by permission of Nature Picture Library. Copyright by Uri Golman. Reprinted by permission.

Teacher think-aloud. Figure 1. One page of article for demonstration with my notes.

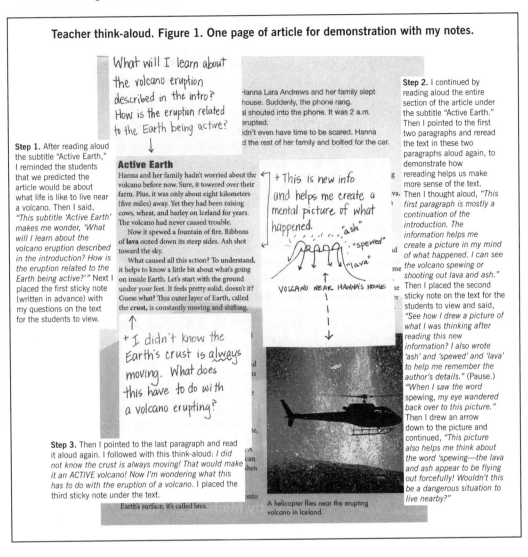

FIGURE 6.1. *(cont.)*

write your notes in front of your students as you think aloud; either way, I find my thinking-aloud demonstration to be more effective if I prepare in advance.

- **Copy "coding" bookmarks.** Make a copy of the codes for each student to use during guided and independent practice. This copy can be used in multiple lessons and may serve as a bookmark.

- **Collect materials,** including the following: sticky notes (several for each student in the group) and one piece of blank paper (8″×11″ or larger) for each student.

Suggestions for Implementation of the Lesson

1. **Establish the purpose of the lesson.** These are the objectives of the lesson that can be posted for students to view and/or be stated aloud in student-friendly terms:

   - Self-monitor continuously while reading (i.e., stay focused on what you are understanding and learning while reading).

   - As we read, consider different aspects of what you do as a reader to self-monitor, such as thinking about what you already know or what is new information as well as thinking about what you don't understand or what you are wondering.

   - As you self-monitor, begin to determine what is important to remember and what the author's central idea appears to be.

2. **Introduce the text, and activate background knowledge about the topic.**

   - If the text is on an unfamiliar subject, engage the students in a short background-knowledge building experience; this might be as simple as talking to any nearby peers about what anyone already knows about the topic or subject.

   - If the text is on a familiar topic, then introduce the texts you have chosen, and explain how these texts are related to the content-area unit of study. You might spend a few minutes reviewing with the students what they already know about the topic.

   - Provide time for the students to browse the text, and then systematically preview the text to make predictions about what they will learn and the author's central idea(s). This might be done as a whole group or in small groups, depending on the needs of your students.

3. **Explain the necessity of self-monitoring while reading, introduce the coding method, and demonstrate with a teacher think-aloud.**

   - *Explain self-monitoring.* Use student-friendly language to explain what might seem like an abstract concept. For example, you might say:

     Have you ever been reading a text and your mind starts to wander? Then you finish a section of the text, but you really have no idea what you have been reading? [Wait for the students to think about what you have said, and then respond.] To avoid this problem, we have to self-monitor or keep ourselves focused on what we are understanding and learning while we read. One method of doing this is to "code" our thinking as we go.

- *Introduce the coding method.* To introduce the coding method, you might say:

  > You can code your thinking by stopping at the end of a portion of text and asking yourself a few important questions.

  Visually project the codes and related prompts for students to view, and explain each one; at this point, you might also pass out copies of the codes to the students individually. As noted previously, these are the codes I introduce to students:

  +   This is new information.

  *   I already knew this information.

  ?   I wonder . . . or I don't understand . . .

  !   Wow! This is interesting!

- *Project the sample of text* you prepared in advance for the group to view (or, in the case of small-group instruction, ask the students to look at their own copy of the text). While the students may be reading at different levels, I have found that there is enough support during this type of interaction for all students to engage, either by listening and watching or by listening while engaged in shared reading. When they move to guided practice, they will need texts at their individual instructional level.

- *Read aloud and think aloud.* Read aloud a section of text, and then demonstrate rereading and stopping to self-monitor after each "chunk" of text. Think aloud about a particular fact or group of facts in the text and how one of the codes might apply to what you are thinking (i.e., you already knew this information; or, this is new information; or, you did not understand a portion of it; or, you thought this information was very interesting).

- *Engage in modeled writing.* As you think aloud about how you used a code to help you self-monitor, write on the visually projected text or sticky note or place a sticky note with your thoughts already written on the text for the students to view (see Figure 6.1).

4. **Engage the students in guided practice with the teacher as coach.**
   - *Continue to discuss the sample text.* Ask the students to join you in a shared think-aloud, and read aloud the next section of text.
   - *Engage in the shared writing of codes and notes.* Solicit responses from the students, and write on the visually projected text or sticky notes. Put the contributing student's initials next to each response.

5. Encourage independent or partner practice, and continue to coach.

- *Direct the students to "try out coding."* Ask the students to, first, read one section of text independently or with a partner and then code it and take notes. Check in frequently with those students who may need more modeling or scaffolding. Ask the students to share, in pairs or groups of three, how they self-monitored by using "codes" and the knowledge they gained from the text.

- *Confer during continued practice.* This is where the bulk of the lesson should occur. As the students continue reading additional sections of the text and taking notes, engage individuals or pairs of students in conversations. These conversations should provide you with many opportunities to coach for deeper understanding of how to monitor for understanding. As in previous chapters, I have listed some likely scenarios that might develop and the language that teachers can use to move their students forward (see Table 6.1).

TABLE 6.1. Common Conferring Scenarios and Suggestions for Coaching

Scenario	Coaching language and actions
The student has written several "I already knew" codes with his or her notes.	Prompt: "So, how does what you already knew help you understand the central idea in this article?" and, if needed, "Tell me more."
The student has written several thoughts but has not written any questions.	Possible prompts: • "So, what were you wondering as you read this?" • "Was there a tricky part of the text that you didn't understand very well?" and then "What did you do to help yourself understand that part better?" or "What could you do to help yourself understand that part better?" Be prepared to teach at the point of need. The student might identify specific obstacles to understanding, such as encountering unfamiliar vocabulary words or numerous other problems.
The student has written notes about running text but not about the features.	Possible prompts: • "When you looked at this diagram (or picture or chart, etc.), what were you thinking in your mind?" • "How did this help you understand the text better?"
The student has written a variety of notes about several aspects of the text and features and needs to move toward synthesizing the information written on the notes.	Possible prompts: • "It looks like you are thinking carefully about what you are reading. When you look across your notes, what are you thinking might be the central idea in this article?" • "When we first looked at this text, we predicted it would be about [*fill in the blank*]. What are you thinking now?" and then "Why do you think so?"

6. **Close with a conversation about the synthesis of new information and reflections on the strategic reading that was accomplished.**

- *Regroup.*
- *Introduce or review using the framed photograph analogy to synthesize information on sticky notes.* Ask the students to place their sticky notes in the middle of a blank sheet of paper. (If needed, they can layer the sticky notes in order to fit them all in the allotted space, or you can even use larger sheets of paper.) Next, ask them to draw a frame around the notes, reminding them of the picture frame analogy (introduced in Chapter 3). Ask the students to reread (and if necessary rearrange) all of their notes, synthesize their thinking, and write sentences about the author's main idea(s) in the frame around the edge (see Figures 6.2 and 6.3).

  The first time you engage in this activity, you may need to model for the students or think aloud together about the central ideas in the text. Place a blank piece of paper under the document camera or a transparency on the overhead and model drawing a frame around the edge of the paper (1- to 2-inches thick). Then place the sticky notes (or a copy of sticky notes copied on a transparency) in the middle of the frame and engage the students in a shared think-aloud about the central ideas in the text—as conveyed in their notes. Gradually, over time, the students should be encouraged to do this independently and then to share their thoughts with a small group of peers. (See Figure 6.3 for an example of one student's framed notes.)

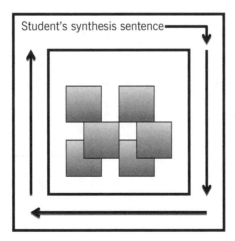

FIGURE 6.2. Layout for synthesis frame and sticky notes.

FIGURE 6.3. Example of fifth-grade student's framed notes.

- *Finish the lesson* by having a conversation about the benefits of self-monitoring as you read. Questions you might pose include:

   How did self-monitoring help you today?

   Why is self-monitoring an important practice to engage in while reading?

   How might you use this practice when you are by yourself and you are reading an unfamiliar informational text?

   What do you need to work on to improve your self-monitoring?

7. **Assess and plan your next lesson.**
   - *Read and assess the students' work.* Table 6.2 includes descriptions of students' coded notes. This continuum is applicable to third- through eighth-grade students. If the students are engaged in reading instructional-level texts, they are capable of responding at all of the levels below, regardless of age. Their notes may reveal thinking at more than one level. This continuum is a tool for grasping the general level of thinking revealed by the students and for generating ideas on how you might move individuals or small groups forward. Use the continuum to assess and determine an objective to focus on in the next lesson. What can you model to deepen their understanding of self-monitoring? See suggestions for follow-up instruction in Table 6.2.
   - Choose examples that reflect effective self-monitoring or that support your objective to share during the follow-up lesson.

■ Lesson 2: Using Students' Coded Notes to Continue Teaching for Self-Monitoring

After the lesson described in Figure 6.1 using the article "KABOOM!" from *National Geographic Explorer! Pathfinder* (Ruane, 2010), I looked through the students' coded notes from that lesson and noticed several categories of responses. I also read the students' framed sentences—the sentences describing the author's central ideas. When I was finished, I chose five examples of coded notes and two examples of central idea sentences to share in a follow-up mini-lesson the next day with the same class. My purpose was to highlight what each student did well as a model for their peers and then ask the students to use their peers' notes as a model for more attentive self-monitoring and note taking.

TABLE 6.2. Stages of Development in Taking Notes about Self-Monitoring

Stage of development	Description of student's written responses	Suggestions for follow-up instruction
Attempting	*Coded notes*—The student writes notes restating facts from the text and may include a low-level response like "I learned that . . ." with no elaboration. The student relies on the use of just one or two codes for responding. Examples: <table><tr><td>+ The platypus has electrical sensors in its nostrils.</td><td>+ The Australian frilled lizard can grow to be a meter long.</td></tr></table> *Theme notes*—The student writes a single fact from the text or a general statement that reveals only a surface-level understanding of the topic. Examples: One (cassowary) can kill with one kick! To give you information about what's happening and facts about volcanoes.	• During a follow-up lesson, check in with the student during guided practice. Engage in a shared think-aloud about a chunk of text; be prepared to share your own thinking about the text that demonstrates using more than one way to self-monitor (i.e., using more than one code). • During a mini-lesson, model aloud thinking through what a fact or particular vocabulary word means. It is likely that the students (whose notes are shown at left) do not understand fully what an "electrical sensor" is or how long a "meter" might be. For these students I would think aloud about what I do and do not understand about these terms; I would sketch what I am thinking and write questions about what I do not understand. • As part of these mini-lessons, I would also think aloud about how understanding these facts about these animals helps me think about the author's central idea and what I am beginning to think may be the central idea.
Approaching	*Coded notes*—The student writes notes that reveal the construction of meaning and some level of thinking that reaches beyond the text. The student uses multiple codes and adds personal responses that reveal engagement with the text, like "I never knew . . ." and "I'm surprised . . ." The student also begins to identify what he or she does not understand in the text. Examples: <table><tr><td>Wow! That doesn't even look like an animal. It blends in good to get easy food.</td><td>Could the secretary bird be related to cranes?</td></tr></table> *Theme notes*—The student writes a statement that narrows in on the specific topic of the text or writes a statement that reveals an emerging understanding of the theme. Examples: This passage informs you of facts about animals like how they defend themselves. To inform the readers about how animals might look weird but how great they are.	• During a mini-lesson, ask the class to view examples of students' notes that ask questions and affirm what the student is doing well; then think aloud about how you might write an additional note about the answer to the question, including information you read further along in the text or a note saying that you did not locate the information to answer the question. • During a follow-up mini-lesson, specifically demonstrate *not* understanding part of a text by reading aloud a tricky part of the text and thinking aloud about how, if you were a student, your meaning might break down. You can then model a number of "fix-up" strategies for repairing meaning, such as rereading or thinking about the meanings of unfamiliar words. Model writing on a sticky note about this experience and what you did to figure out the author's meaning. • A short mini-lesson might focus on writing proper nouns versus pronouns. (See the first student example in "Coded Notes.") • Each time you think aloud, make a connection to how what you are doing helps you think about the author's central idea. Make clear the difference between a topic of the text and a central idea (theme). *(cont.)*

128

TABLE 6.2. *(cont.)*

Stage of development	Description of student's written responses	Suggestions for follow-up instruction
Meeting	*Coded notes*—The student reveals thinking that involves the application and/or analysis of ideas. The student uses codes flexibly, sometimes resorting to different kinds of coding or note taking, such as sketching. The student may identify tricky parts of the text and write about what he or she did to "fix up" the meaning. In the example below, a student wrote a question on the first sticky note; then, when he read on and determined the answer, he wrote on a second sticky note.	• Engage the students in a mini-lesson focused on elaboration. • Move students into writing responses using their codes as notes. Confer one-on-one or in a small group. Ask the student to elaborate orally on what he or she is thinking regarding notes written for a particular code. As the student talks, jot down notes on what he or she is saying; next, paraphrase aloud what you heard. Ask him or her to extend the response in writing, and leave the notes you took with the student.

Examples:

? How is lightning reacting with lava and a volcanic eruption?	+ Static electricity builds up in the ashes and forms lightning.

Theme notes—The student writes statements that identify a clear theme.

Examples:

I think the big idea was people in Marsabit have to work very hard for a small amount of unclean water and most people just turn on a faucet.

Stage of development	Description of student's written responses	Suggestions for follow-up instruction
Exceeding	*Coded notes*—The student uses codes flexibly and elaborates, responding in a variety of ways. Many notes tie into an emerging theme. The notes reveal an evaluation of the facts or ideas shared in the text.	• See the recommendations for "meeting." • Make sure the text being read is not below the instructional level of the student, and then move the student toward writing extended responses while using his or her notes.

Examples:

I believe Hanna was caring for her cows, but leaving 60? I mean that's 60 lives lost!	! Wow. It seems like we waste a lot of water and it's very easy to get water compared to other countries.

Theme notes—The student identifies and elaborates on the theme.

Example:

I think the author wrote this article to persuade people to save water and use it when you really need it. I think that this is a very important topic because we use a lot of water. We use it daily and it is also something that many people need.

Description of the Lesson

I began the mini-lesson by restating the importance of self-monitoring. Then I made sure everyone had a coding method bookmark and asked the students to think–pair–share with a partner to review the coding method. Next I placed each student's written notes, one at a time, on the document camera and thought aloud about what each response revealed to me. I've now shared how I thought aloud about two of the responses in Table 6.3. For the purposes of sharing with

TABLE 6.3. Using Students' Notes to Teach

Student example	Teacher think-aloud
Anna's response:	I wanted the students to consider how Anna had thought beyond the facts the author had shared.
✦ I just found out that the Volcano has not eruptid since 1812 thats a very very long time ago!	I placed her work on the document camera, pointed to this particular sticky note, and said: Notice in this student's note that she included not just the specific fact she learned while reading, but also she stopped to think about what this fact tells us, namely, it's been a long time since this volcano erupted. I'm thinking she was also considering that this might be why the people living nearby were not worried on a regular basis about the volcano erupting.
Luke's response:	I wanted the students to notice how Luke had written a question and then an answer.
? How is lightning reacting with lava and a Volcanic eruption.	I placed his work on the document camera and said: Take a moment to look at the thinking this student has shared in these notes. How did he go about self-monitoring? [Pause and then solicit answers or continue thinking aloud.] I noticed that on the first sticky note he wrote a question. [I quickly removed the student's work and placed a page of the article on the camera—with an illustration and caption.] I'm guessing that he had read the caption that said "Lightning sparks in the ash plume of the eruption" and then looked at the picture with all of the ash in the sky and a streak of lightning in the middle of it. [Pause.] Then he must have continued reading and located the answer in the text, which is what he has written on the second note.
+ Static electricity builds up in the ashes and forms lightning	

you, I have included only the portion of the student's work that I highlighted during the mini-lesson. During the actual mini-lesson, I placed the student's entire work product on the document camera for the whole class to view. I requested the student's permission in advance, of course, and I'm always careful not to divulge whose work I am talking about when I think aloud in front of the group. As another teaching option, you might consider inviting in advance the student whose work you are sharing to come up and co-think aloud with you, as well.

After this short presentation, I asked the students to read a second article, self-monitor by writing coded notes, and then synthesize the content. I moved around to confer with individual students whose written notes were mostly at the attempting level during the first lesson. We wrapped up by sharing our thinking in small groups.

Example of a Student's Growth after the Second Lesson

It is remarkable how much a simple approach to following up—like sharing students' work and describing explicitly what each student did to construct meaning from the text—can do to move students forward. When Danuta read the first article about the volcano eruption, she wrote sentences on eight sticky notes that started with "I never knew" or "I already knew." She followed with facts stated almost directly from the text, like "I already knew that the Earth's mantle lies under the crust." She also asked two questions but did not follow with answers. In the synthesis frame, she wrote the following two sentence fragments: "To give you information on volcanoes" and "To inform you on the volcano that erupted in Iceland." Her responses revealed that she was attempting to self-monitor but still needed further instruction.

After the follow-up mini-lesson, Danuta read the article "Thirsty Planet" (Geiger, 2010) about how water is a limited resource that all living things need ready access to in order to survive. Figure 6.4 shows her response along with the additional sticky notes she attached to the back of her paper. As you read, notice the variety of responses and that most of her notes are focused on how animals and plants use or conserve water. She is still stating many facts, but she is including responses that reveal thinking beyond the text (see the comment about "camels"). She also seems to be keeping track of her thinking as she reads (see the two "birch tree" notes). In addition, she seems to be contrasting new information with old beliefs (in her "tadpoles" comment), and she is asking (and sometimes answering) questions about key vocabulary words (*conserve* and *condense*). Her three theme sentences reveal her thoughtful consideration of the author's central

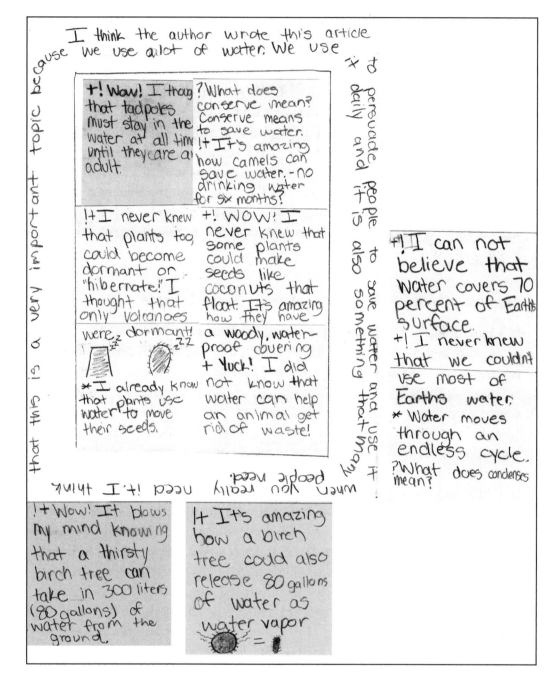

FIGURE 6.4. Danuta's response after the second lesson.

ideas and the implications for the reader. She has clearly moved beyond merely reaching out to self-monitor and now is much more in control of her understanding as a result.

■ What's Next?

We do not wish to have students "burn out" as a result of excessive coding. Rather, we just want them to understand conceptually (preferably without such devices as the coding bookmark) what it means to self-monitor, to be aware of what does and does not make sense, and to use fix-up strategies whenever meaning starts to break down. Step in and step back. Observe when your students are successfully self-monitoring their reading and perhaps don't need to "code" their thinking. However, be ready at all times to pull the coding bookmarks out again—perhaps to tackle a more difficult text, or even as an occasional reminder of the basics of self-monitoring.

When students are just beginning to be more aware of their thinking and starting to self-monitor more consistently and efficiently, you are then all set to introduce a more rigorous way of thinking about how to read a text—namely, reading to determine what is important at the sentence, paragraph, and section level. In Chapter 7, I describe how to demonstrate to students what this looks like in practice and how to engage them most efficiently and effectively in their quest to determine what's really important in the text.

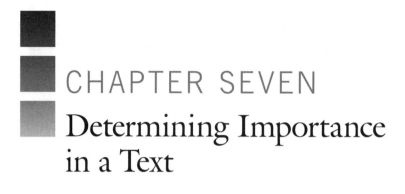

CHAPTER SEVEN
Determining Importance in a Text

Even when our students actively self-monitor while reading, they still struggle to identify key details that support the author's central ideas. Many times, when a student is asked to write a summary of the central ideas in a text and include supporting evidence, the student will write every single fact he or she remembers or just the opposite—the last fact read. Teaching students how to determine the key words or phrases that reveal the really significant ideas in the text requires extraordinary practice, patience, and tenacity. In this chapter, I describe how to teach the student to begin to determine what is truly important at the sentence, paragraph and section levels, how to take notes, and then how to write a summary. I follow with suggestions for teaching specific text structures and also for how to help students strategically read feature-dense texts.

■ Consider Your Students' Strengths and Needs

What have you noticed about your students' ability to determine what is important while reading informational texts?

- When students confer with you:
  - Do they tend to share just the last fact they read in a text?
  - Do they have to look back through the text to remember what they read?
  - Do they share "wow" facts, but not necessarily those that contribute to understanding the author's main ideas?
  - Can they speak in specific terms about what in the text underlies the author's central ideas?

- When students write about what they have read:
  - Do they include facts or information from multiple parts of the text that are just listed or linked in a way that lacks cohesion?
  - Do they include facts drawn primarily from the end of the text?
  - Do they focus on facts or information from their own background knowledge rather than from the text they read?
  - Do they simply recite facts they read with no clear purpose or explanation for why they are including so much information in their response?
  - Do they copy from the text?
  - Do they write coherently about how the author organized information in the text to convey his or her central idea(s)?

How do we help our students move beyond what we are observing? We need to start by visualizing what proficient readers should be able to do when determining what is important. By the end of the eighth grade, according to the CCSS (2010), a student should be able to "determine a central idea of a text and analyze its development over the course of the text, including its relationship to support ideas as well as provide an objective summary of the text." If we unpack this particular standard, students in grades 3–8 should be able to do the following with increasingly difficult texts:

- Determine which key words or phrases in a text reveal the author's central ideas.

- Identify other key words or phrases that lead to important supporting details.

- Explain why certain details support the author's central idea(s).

- Combine key words or phrases in a coherent or logically consistent way to create a credible and objectively correct oral or written summary.

■ Where to Start?
Introducing the "Making Pasta" Analogy

The main lesson described below introduces students to the task of determining what is important by means of the "making pasta" analogy described in Chapter 1. Following the description of this lesson, I have included suggestions for applying both this analogy and the use of foldable notes to texts characterized by such text structures as compare-and-contrast and cause-and-effect as well as texts so dense with features that they are frequently difficult for students to deal with. Other analogies can be used, such as mining for gold, weeding a garden, and the like. Choose an analogy that your students will find the most useful, as the instructional practices described with the pasta analogy can also be applied to the use of any of these analogies as well.

Starting with an analogy (say, making pasta) creates a concrete image for students of how they can go about determining what is important. Most intermediate- and middle-grade students can describe to you the procedure for making pasta. The steps include adding the pasta to boiling water, draining the pasta, and then eating the pasta. Frequently, students who describe this process will leave out the step of draining the water, taking for granted that you know this already. I always ask the students: "What would happen if we ate the water with the pasta? Not so good, huh?" This is the metaphor for determining what is important: the author has pasta words and phrases in a text and "water" words and phrases. The water is important, of course, because it makes the pasta soft and edible. In the end, though, what readers need to eat and digest are the author's pasta words or phrases—the language in the text that identifies the author's central ideas and supporting details.

These ideas for lessons are especially effective with small groups, but I have implemented them with whole classes as well. Regardless of the group size, the critical component of both lessons is the teacher's preparation. The teacher needs to read the text carefully well in advance of the instruction; take notes, identifying the words and phrases that are most important; and then create a credible and accurate summary with those words and phrases. Doing this prepares you for the presentation and think-aloud, for the guided practice, and for any conferring you do during the independent practice portion of the lesson. See Box 7.1 for an example of notes I took in preparation for a specific lesson and for a description of my think-aloud and guided practice with the students.

BOX 7.1. Sample Teacher Think-Aloud and Guided Practice

HOW TO IDENTIFY KEY WORDS AND PHRASES IN A TEXT AND THEN WRITE A SUMMARY

The objective of this lesson was to identify an author's central ideas and supporting details in a text called *Animal Adaptations* (Winkler, 2004); I chose a two-page section of the text, titled "Aardvarks in Action," that described the aardvark's food-related adaptations. Take a moment to read this text in the left-hand column on pages 138–140. Each student had a large sheet of blank paper folded into quarters. They were told to take notes on the first quarter of the sheet during my think-aloud. After my presentation, they were to read and take notes on three additional sections of text during guided and independent practice. In advance, I read the text closely and wrote my own notes (see the figure below for the notes I took to prepare for the lesson as I studied the text).

Aardvark in Action pp8-9
adaptations

aardvark

termites

snout

termite mound hard
        as brick

strong legs & sharp claws

bristles, dust

tough skin protects

long sticky tongue

Diverse Defenses -p 10-11

prey
predator

ways to defend themselves

Australian frilled lizard

        frill
        hiss

South America 3 banded armadillo
        tight ball

work together

Devious Disguises -p 10-11

avoid predator's attention

camouflage

leaf butterfly

looper-part of a flower

mimicry
        hover flies look like wasps

Toadally cool facts -p 13

live everywhere

has hot environments
    desert, toads & frogs
    going dormant, underground

seal in moisture

rain - comes to surface

TEACHER THINK-ALOUD

When I began my think-aloud, I had already introduced the text, engaged in a short discussion to review what the students had already learned in their content-area unit on adaptations, and observed while they browsed through the text. After introducing the making pasta metaphor, I began thinking aloud about how to determine the relative importance of the various facts and ideas in the text. The table below includes my think-aloud (in the right-hand column) about what I was doing as a reader as I read the section heading and the first two paragraphs of the chosen text (in the left-hand column).

Text from *Animal Adaptations* (each student had a copy of this book)	Teacher think-aloud (the words I said during the think-aloud)
Step 1	
	Before reading I said:
	Let me show you how I determined what were important words or phrases in the text.
Aardvarks in Action (p. 8)	After reading aloud the heading "Aardvarks in Action," I reminded the students that we predicted the text would help us learn more about animal adaptations. Then I said:
	This heading, "Aardvarks in Action," makes me ask the question "What will I learn about aardvarks and their adaptations? I'm also thinking this question is related to the author's central idea—something about the aardvark's food-related adaptations.
	I wrote the heading on the chart paper (see figure at end of box).
Step 2	
One way or another, all animals need to eat. So, it's not surprising that many adaptations help animals find and consume food. The aardvark, a mammal that lives in African forests and grasslands, provides great examples of food-related adaptations. (p. 8)	I continued by reading aloud the entire section. Then I pointed to the first paragraph, reread the text in this paragraph again, and said:
	I am thinking this is mostly an introduction, except that when I think about my question "What will I learn about an aardvark's adaptations?," and that I know adaptations are traits that help an animal survive, the word help really jumped out at me, and then the words just after that—animals find and consume food—jumped out at me. Animals have to find and eat food to survive. I'm thinking this section is going to be about the aardvark's adaptations that specifically help it find and eat its food. Let me read and think about the next paragraph with this in mind.
	On the chart paper I wrote "food-related adaptations" below the words *aardvarks in action* (see the figure at the end of the box).
Step 3	
An aardvark eats insects, especially termites. To find termites, it prowls by night, sniffing the ground with its powerful, pig-like snout. Sooner or later, the aardvark finds a termite	I read the second paragraph aloud again (see text at left), and then I read each sentence aloud again, stopping to think aloud after each sentence about the pasta words or important facts the author wants me to remember.

mound, or nest. That's when things get interesting. (p. 8)

My think-aloud sounded like the following:

"An aardvark eats insects, especially termites." *Since I think I'm reading about adaptations of the aardvark that have to do with eating, I am going to write down termites—because the termites are the aardvark's food.*

"To find termites, it prowls by night, sniffing the ground with its powerful, pig-like snout." One word jumps out at me here: snout; the snout is the physical trait the aardvark is using to find termites.

I wrote "snout" on the chart paper.

I continued rereading aloud.

"Sooner or later, the aardvark finds a termite mound, or nest." I am wondering how the aardvark's snout will help him get into the mound. I'm going to write down mound as an important word.

"That's when things get interesting." When I read this, I didn't learn anything about adaptations. I think the author is just trying to get me to read more, to pique my interest.

GUIDED PRACTICE

At this point, the students and I shifted into guided practice. The table below shows the rest of the text I used for guided practice, the key words or phrases the students and I identified together, and some notes about our conversation.

Text from *Animal Adaptations*	Key words or phrases we identified and notes about our conversations
Termite mounds look like giant sand castles. To build them, the insects use a mixture of soil, sand, and saliva. When it dries, the mixture is hard as a brick. The mound's sturdy walls keep out most animals. But not aardvarks. (p. 8)	In my notes, I had written "hard as brick," but the students actually decided not to include any words or phrases from this paragraph. This makes sense because the paragraph does not answer the question that is the purpose for their reading. It explains further about the termite's mound, but it does not give any information about the aardvark's physical traits or adaptations.
Equipped with strong legs and sharp claws, an aardvark rips termite mounds right open. **Bristles**, or stiff hairs, in its nose keep the aardvark from breathing in dust as it digs. (p. 9)	• *sharp claws* • *bristles*

You can imagine how termites respond when their home is demolished. Special termites, called soldiers, fiercely attack the aardvark. But the aardvark's tough skin protects it. (p. 9)

- *tough skin*

To eat, the aardvark relies on its tongue, which can stretch out more than a foot. The aardvark's sticky tongue traps a tasty serving of termites. Getting that meal took hard work—and many different adaptations. (p. 9)

- *long tongue*

After we determined these key words and phrases, we engaged in the shared writing of a summary paragraph for this section of the text. Collaboratively, we wrote the following:

Aardvarks have food-related adaptations to eat termites. They demolish termite mounds with pig-like snouts and sharp claws. The aardvark's tough skin protects it from attacking termites. Finally their sticky tongue helps it eat. The aardvark's food-related adaptations are interesting and unique.

Depending on the amount of time you have with your whole class or small group, you can stop at this point or continue to independent practice. During a second lesson with this group, the students continued reading in this book and taking notes about other animal adaptations.

See the figure below for the chart paper on which I wrote notes during the teacher think-aloud and the shared think-aloud. On the left, we checked off or crossed out notes as we used those ideas to compose the summary sentences on the right. Notice how the words listed on the left are woven into the summary.

▨ Focus Lesson: Identifying Key Phrases That Are Important

Suggestions for Lesson Preparation and Text Study

- **Choose a text** (preferably related to the content-area unit of study) that is well written and that lends itself to student's easily identifying the author's central ideas and supporting details. Be highly selective: the text you choose is one way to scaffold for strategic reading by the student. Later on, more complex texts or ones that are less well written may be used.

- **Study the text and take notes.**

- **Prepare a think-aloud** that includes reading aloud a paragraph or section of text and thinking aloud about why you would pick particular words or phrases to include in your notes.

- **Collect materials** including the following: two pieces of chart paper or butcher paper large enough for students to view the shared writing of notes, thick-tipped markers for shared writing, one large sheet of paper for each student (preferably 11″×17″), and a set of the text being used.

Suggestions for Implementation of the Lesson

1. **Establish the purpose of the lesson.** These are the objectives of the lesson that can be posted for students to view and explained further by the teacher:
   - Read a text closely and determine the author's central ideas and the details that support these ideas.
   - Combine the central ideas and supporting details into a summary that makes sense.
   - *Optional*—Learn new information that answers essential questions in the content-area unit of study.

2. **Introduce the text and set the purpose for reading.** The introduction needs to involve activating background knowledge and making predictions about the author's central idea(s) as a way to set a purpose for reading. If you have time, ask the students to read the whole text or give them 5–10 minutes to read independently. If this is an instructional-level text, they will not be able to read the text proficiently, but this gives them time to begin grappling with the ideas in the text without interruption. Engage in a shared think-aloud, with the students predicting aloud what they think the central ideas will be

and why (based on their preview of the text). Remind them that this serves as their purpose for reading—to affirm or adjust their predictions of the author's central idea(s) as they read.

3. **Explain the strategy of determining what is important and the pasta metaphor and demonstrate with a teacher think-aloud.**

   - *Start with a teaser.* You might say the following:

     > Do you ever struggle with figuring out what is important in a text? [Pause.] Do you ever struggle with summarizing what you have read about in a text? [Pause.] Do you sometimes just want to copy from the book? [Pause.] Or do you write about the last fact you read? [Pause.] Today we are going to be talking about how to determine what is really important in a text, take notes about what you are thinking, and then write a summary using those notes.

   - *Explain the metaphor and its purpose.*

     > Let's start with a metaphor. Tell me about making pasta. First you boil water, right? Then you add the pasta and when it is cooked, you eat the pasta, correct? [Pause for student response.] Oh, yes. You need to drain the water from the pasta, and *then* you eat the pasta. It is the same way when we read. The author has included both "water" and "pasta" words and phrases in a text. The pasta in an informational text is the important facts or points the author wants us to remember. What the author wants is for us to eat and digest the pasta words—the water words are not as important; the water words or phrases help make the pasta, but what is important is for us to eat and digest the pasta words or phrases.

     During this explanation, you might have a picture of pasta or a set of pictures that shows the process of making pasta; sometimes I sketch the pasta-making process as I discuss it with the students. This is especially important if you are working with striving readers or English learners who need additional scaffolding to understand how this metaphor applies to reading.

   - *Read aloud a section of the text and think aloud.* Read aloud from one heading to the next, and then reread the whole section to demonstrate how to determine the importance of the words used and the ideas developed. Think aloud about which words or phrases you think are particularly significant and why (see the sample think-aloud in Box 7.1). Continue doing this until you have thought aloud about the entire section of the text.

- *Engage in modeled writing of notes as you go.* As you think aloud, write the words or phrases on the chart paper for the students to view.
- *Engage in modeled writing of summary sentence.* Think aloud about how the words and phrases listed all support a central idea; compose a sentence out loud to "try out" putting the words together in a coherent way. Revise aloud as needed, and then write the summary sentence. Reread the sentence, and revise or edit as needed.

4. **Engage the students in guided practice with the teacher as coach.**
   - *Engage the students in a shared think-aloud.* Read aloud another section of the text, and elicit key words and phrases from the students. Some students may not be ready to practice with you and may need you to think aloud for another section of the text. Gradually pull them in by asking them to read the next paragraph silently and then to share "pasta" (i.e., key) words or phrases that "jump out at them" as important. Ask them to explain why they think these words are important, and, if they hesitate, prompt them to think about their purpose for reading. The students will not always pick the words or phrases that you may have picked when you prepared, but this learning experience is not about "getting it right." Instead, ask the students to justify why they think these words they chose are important to remember, and then prompt them to think about how the words provide information related to their purpose for reading.
   - *Engage in the shared writing of notes as you go.* To help keep track and to motivate your students, write each student's initials next to his or her contribution as you take notes, listing the key words and phrases each one chose and justified.
   - *Engage in the shared writing of a summary sentence or two.* Think aloud with the students about how they might combine the key words and phrases to form a summary sentence.

5. **Encourage independent practice and continue to confer.** This is when the students read further in the text, identifying the key words or phrases that are important to the purpose of their reading. During the lesson with the fourth graders, there were three additional sections in the same chapter of the book *Animal Adaptations.* They read and took notes about these sections during the independent practice. Each section started with a heading and explained further various adaptations. For each section of text, they identified the key words and phrases and then wrote summary sentences.

Table 7.1 describes some likely scenarios that might develop when using this approach with students and the language you should use to prompt the student's thinking in such situations.

6. **Close with a conversation on the synthesis of content and reflections on the strategic reading accomplished.**

7. **Assess student learning and plan your next lesson.** Take time to look through the students' lists of key words and summaries. Table 7.2 includes descriptions of what you might observe in students' notes as they develop greater facility with this strategy.

TABLE 7.1. Conferring Scenarios and Suggestions for Coaching

Scenario	Coaching language and actions
The student is looking to see what others are writing and seems unclear about his or her purpose for reading.	Prompt: "Tell me a little about what you are planning to do to determine what is important."
	If the student hesitates, remind him or her to preview and then predict, or think aloud on the spot with your own preview and prediction. Next, talk with the student about his or her purpose for reading, and how it is determined by the prediction.
	Think aloud about a portion of the text, modeling how you would determine which words or phrases are most important.
	Ask the student to think aloud and take notes as he or she reads and to share what seems most important. Have a conversation that explores why these particular words or phrases are important.
The student is writing too much information from the text in his or her notes or is copying directly from the text.	Prompt the student as follows, and be prepared to step in and think aloud as needed: • "Tell me why you have chosen these words or phrases." • "Which one of these words you have written down would be enough to communicate the author's central idea?" • "How can you say this in your own words? What does the author mean in this sentence?"
The student is writing words and phrases from the text that seem clearly tied to a central idea.	Check in with this student, and affirm the positive aspects of his or her work. Prompt: "Tell me how you chose these particular words."
	If appropriate, prompt the student to think about how he or she will combine the ideas into a written summary. Prompt: "What are you going to do to figure out how to start a written summary?"
The student has started writing but does not appear to be thinking clearly about how to combine ideas successfully from his or her notes.	Prompt the student, and be prepared to step in and think aloud: "How could you combine some of these ideas from your notes?"
	Remind the student of the shared writing that the group did. Engage the student in a conversation about how the group went about deciding how to combine ideas. Remind the student of such words as *and, also, such as,* and *for example* that help the writer connect ideas.

TABLE 7.2. Stages of Development in the Student's Determining What Is Important and in Summarizing

Stage of development	Description of the student's responses (oral and written)	Suggestions for follow-up instruction
Attempting	• The words listed may seem random, as though the student does not understand conceptually what it means to determine what is important. The words listed do not give a clear sense of a central idea. • Too much information is listed. • The summary may include language copied directly from the text.	• Meet in a one-on-one conference with the student or a group of students with similar needs, and engage in guided practice focused on previewing the text and making predictions about the author's central idea. Model for the students beginning to read the text with that central idea in mind. • Engage in a think-aloud with particular sentences that would "just be easy to copy." Think aloud about how, instead of copying, you are going to paraphrase. Explain and write aloud your paraphrase of the text.
Approaching	• The student has a grasp of a central idea, and the words he or she has chosen to list could support that idea. The student is beginning to articulate more clearly why he or she chose these particular words and phrases as important. • The student's summary includes a statement that reveals a central idea, like "Some animals have adaptations to defend themselves." • The student's summary is "list-like" in that it appears that the student worked his or her way down the list of words, writing a sentence for each. • There is some retelling, including too many details, so that the "summary" is almost as long as the text. • The student is starting to share his or her own thinking (which is appropriate if the student has been assigned to a "summary and synthesis"). The student's thoughts may feel "tacked on." For example, the student includes a sentence at the end such as "This was new information to me." • The student's list and summary in some ways include language that describes the content of the features as well as the main text. • The student attempts to orally summarize the text with notes.	• When your students attempt to determine what is important in a new text, engage in a shared think-aloud and shared note taking for the first paragraph or section of the text before they start to work on their own. • With a list of key words or phrases, think aloud and write aloud about how you go about combining certain words or ideas from the list into a sentence. • Create visually accessible images of students' lists and summaries to share. Talk with the students about the strengths of the lists of words and the summaries written.

(cont.)

TABLE 7.2. *(cont.)*

Stage of development	Description of the student's responses (oral and written)	Suggestions for follow-up instruction
Meeting	• The student is easily identifying words and phrases that are clearly tied to a central idea. The student is able to share aloud why he or she chose particular words or phrases. • The student incorporates key words and phrases that are drawn from or inferred from the features. • The student recognizes when key words or phrases in notes are related and successfully combines them to make a point in the summary. • If assigned to summarize *and* synthesize, the student integrates into the summary relevant ideas or facts not directly stated in the text. For example, one student was reading about animals that blend into their surroundings, and he added, "This reminds me of chameleons, who change colors, too." • The student can summarize the text orally to begin a discussion with a small group.	• See the recommendations for "approaching." • Shift to determining what is important in more complex texts. This might include texts that are packed with features and that have less running text. Model and guide as needed. • Shift to determining what is important and synthesizing across multiple texts.
Exceeding	• The student extends the ideas in the text by sharing relevant background knowledge, ideas, or facts not found in the text. In addition, the student explains how these additional ideas combine with the other details to support the author's central idea. • If assigned to do so, the student evaluates how the author's organization of facts and ideas works to convey the central ideas in the text. • The student summarizes text orally and engages in conversation easily about the author's central ideas and more.	• See recommendations for "meeting."

Figure 7.1 presents one example of a student's list and written summary. The student is at the "approaching" (expectations) stage of development for determining what is important. His summary is "list-like" in that he states the central idea, lists facts, and then wraps up with a personal statement. The reader is left to infer how, specifically, the facts support the central idea.

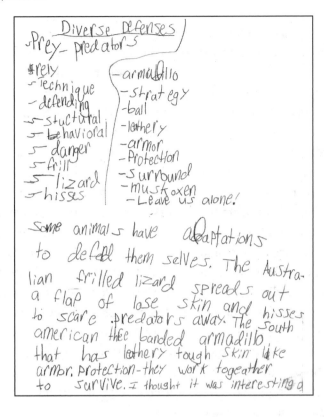

FIGURE 7.1. Example of the written notes of a student at the "approaching" (expectations) stage of development.

■ Determining What Is Important with Texts That Fit a Specific Structure

Correctly identifying a recurrent text structure such as comparison or cause–effect is part of determining what is important. If a student can readily identify a particular text structure, this may help him or her focus better on the author's central ideas and determine what is important at the sentence and paragraph levels. This is when the pasta analogy comes back into play. Text structures commonly referred to in the professional literature and in teaching materials include:

- Description (including definitions and examples).
- Sequence/time order.
- Comparison.
- Cause–effect.
- Problem–solution.

As was noted in Chapter 1, teaching how to spot a specific text structure is valuable only if the student can begin to recognize independently when the author is employing a particular structure at the macro and micro levels. At the macro level, students can recognize when a whole text or section of text is organized around a particular structure. A macro text structure extends beyond the sentence level. For example, a student might be reading a magazine article about an endangered species and how a community is working to save this species. Being able to appreciate that the author has organized his or her ideas by using a problem–solution text structure serves to help the student identify the central idea and determine what is important. Authors may choose to organize the whole text or sections of text by using a particular text structure. In Chapter 1, the example of the text on the digestive system included sections of text written in different text structures: cause–effect, sequence, and description (see Figure 1.1, page 13).

At the micro level, the student needs to be able to recognize when an author is employing a particular structure in a sentence or just a few sentences to make a point or extend the meaning of an idea. Again, think back to Chapter 1, specifically the discussion of eighth-grade world history book (Spielvogel, 2005). There, in describing how anthropologists and archaeologists date human artifacts and fossils, the author employed several different text structures at the micro level within a few paragraphs (see pages 14–16).

To introduce or review particular macro text structures with students, I still employ the pasta analogy and list key words and phrases, but I also use folded blank paper, or "foldables," for students to take notes on. A foldable is a blank piece of paper folded in a certain way by the student to represent the structure of the text. Foldables can be used to record notes or to write responses to the text. They are easy to make because all you need in the way of supplies is blank paper. Figures 7.2–7.4 are examples of foldable notes that serve as concrete visual reminders of the text structure for students. I am not the original creator of any of these. Colleagues have passed these on to me, or I have picked them up from other sources, including books by Dinah Zikes.

Foldable notes have been around for a while, and students say they have fun when you use these during instruction. The trick is in getting the students past the entertaining part sufficiently well for them to understand how the folded notes actually help them visualize and comprehend the structure of the text much better. The foldable can serve as a concrete image of how the author has organized the ideas in the text. If the student recognizes that an author has organized the facts through a sequence of four events, he or she will more easily be able to determine what is important and ultimately to synthesize the information. If the student recognizes that the author is contrasting the butterfly and the moth, he or she will more easily be able to determine what to pay attention to as it relates to the author's central idea.

To teach students how to better understand text structure by using folded notes, I make a model with at least a portion of the notes or written response prepared in advance. The foldable notes in Figure 7.2–7.4 are examples of my models; these notes also help me articulate better when thinking aloud for students. I create a visually accessible image of the text for the students to view and prepare a think-aloud about the words or phrases or sentences I read in the text that indicated to me a particular structure and why.

Sequence/Time-Order Text-Structure Foldable

This is a good foldable if you have a text that is structured by moving from one event to the next. For example, in a short social studies text on the history of Veteran's Day, the author identified four separate dates featuring major events that

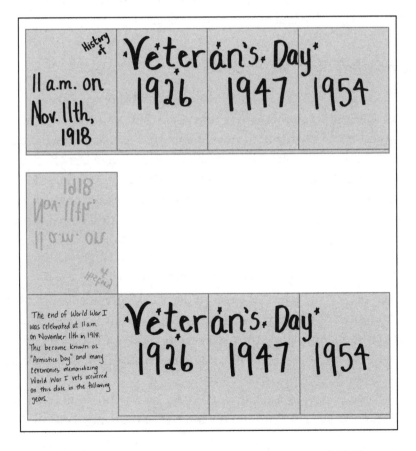

FIGURE 7.2. Sequence/time-order text-structure foldable.

led to the establishment of November 11th as a federal holiday. Students wrote a date on the front of each flap and then described the corresponding event for that date on the inside of the flap. Figure 7.2 shows the model I made to share with the students. I used an 11″ × 17″ sheet of paper to provide more room for written notes. Conceptually, this foldable represents how the text is organized sequentially by date into four main parts.

Directions for making the foldable shown in Figure 7.2.

1. Hold paper so that the longer side is horizontal like a hotdog. Fold the top half of the sheet down, and crease it.
2. Then fold the sheet into quarters, moving from left to right and creasing as you go. Next, unfold the sheet of paper completely.
3. With the paper positioned so that the longer side is horizontal like a hot-dog, cut the three creases between the quarters on only the top half of the paper. Fold the flaps down.
4. Write the name of the event, or the date, or the step in a process on the front of each flap and a description inside.

Comparison Text-Structure Foldable

This foldable is similar to a Venn diagram. Figure 7.3 shows a foldable I prepared with a text that contrasted moths and butterflies. With this foldable, the students can take notes about how the butterflies and moths are alike inside the center section of the foldable. Then they can write about what is unique about the butterfly inside the left-hand section of the foldable and about the moth inside the right-hand section of the text. Conceptually, the foldable represents how the author has looked at the similarities of (the shared center) and the differences (the opposite sides) between these two insects.

Directions for making the foldable shown in Figure 7.3.

1. Hold an 8½″ × 11″ sheet of paper so that the longer side is horizontal. Fold the top half of the paper nearly all the way down (leaving a 1″ margin at the bottom), and crease the paper. Leave the sheet folded.
2. Fold the page into thirds, moving from left to right, and then crease it. Next, unfold the paper.
3. With the paper positioned so the long side is horizontal, cut the two creases between the thirds on the top half of the paper. Fold all three flaps down.

4. On the front of the flaps at the bottom, have the students write the following (from the first flap to the third):
   • Different
   • Same
   • Different

   The students can also draw an image of what they learned on these flaps, as well.

5. On the inside of the left- and right-hand flaps, write a summary or supply bulleted notes or another type of response describing how the concepts are different from each other. Inside the center flap, write about how the concepts are similar.

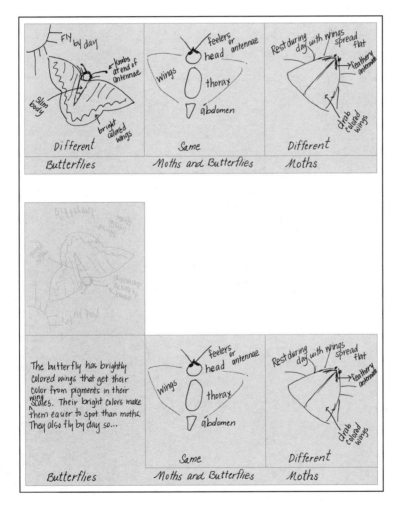

FIGURE 7.3. Comparison text-structure foldable.

Cause–Effect/Problem–Solution Text-Structure Foldable

This foldable is for texts that present a clear problem and solution or a cause and effect. The flap with the problem written on it covers the inside where the solution is described. In preparation for a lesson with eighth graders, I read an article in the magazine *Current Science* and prepared the foldable shown in Figure 7.4. On the "cause" flap, I wrote about the mercury detected in the air in the Pacific Northwest and the evidence that this type of air pollution drifted across the Pacific Ocean from China. Inside the flap, I wrote and sketched about the effects

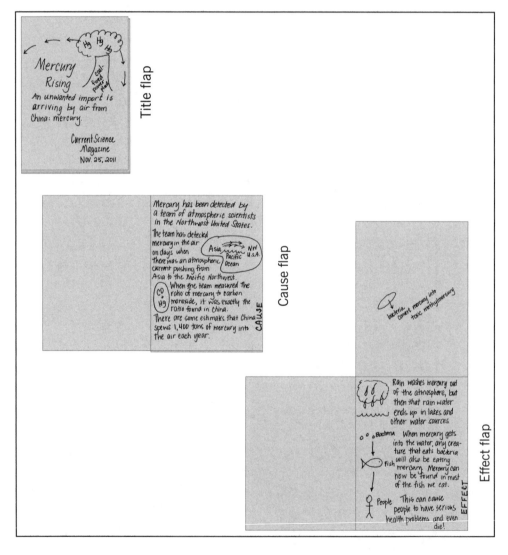

FIGURE 7.4. Cause–effect/problem–solution text-structure foldable.

of this pollution. Conceptually, the cause comes before the effect. In this foldable, the cause is written on the flap that has to be unfolded to see the effects written inside. I had lots of questions after I read this article. I could easily have listed them on another quadrant on the three-quarter book and written a personal response as well.

Directions for making the foldable shown in Figure 7.4.

1. Fold a sheet of 8½″×11″ paper into quadrants, and then unfold it completely.
2. Holding the paper so that the shorter side is horizontal, cut the top left-hand quadrant completely out.
3. Fold the top right-hand quadrant down and then the bottom left-hand quadrant over. This is a three-quarter book.
4. Write the title of the text on the front flap, and illustrate the title.
5. Open the front flap, and write the problem or cause on the right-hand flap (the one that was folded down in step 3).
6. Lift this flap, and on the inside write notes or a response about the effect or solution.
7. Extension: On any of the other blank quadrants or the right-hand quadrant, write a personal response or list questions about the topic you would want to research further.

▨ Teaching with Feature-Dense Texts

Publishers of informational texts have moved from producing texts with hardly any features at all a generation ago to texts that are now packed with features. Even textbooks are overloaded with features these days. The problem is that students frequently just peruse these texts without deepening their knowledge or understanding of the subject of the text. We have to help them understand how to prospect for and then mine the ideas in these types of texts.

Remember those dense feature-packed books in the Kids Discover and *Eyewitness* series published by DK? The student would open the book to any two-page spread and instantly the child's eyes would pop wide open with astonishment at the sheer volume of information being shared. How do you teach for determining what is important with these texts? I was stumped, too, when a fifth-grade teacher presented me with the Kids Discover book *Mesopotamia* (1999) for a demonstration lesson. Then I noticed the Sunday newspaper ads on the kitchen table. Think about one of those multicolored, multipage glossy advertisements for Target. Each page features a particular category of merchandise. On the weekend of the Super Bowl, one page filled with televisions and crockpots and indoor grills was titled "super buys for big game entertaining," and another page with towels and bathroom accessories was titled "soak up the savings" (*Chicago Tribune*, January 29, 2012). The Kids Discover texts are designed the same way. Each page or two-page spread in those texts has a particular focus, and every detail ties in with that particular focus. For example, in the Discover Kids *Mesopotamia* volume, there is a two-page spread titled "Day to Day" (pp. 6–7) that is full of pictures of artifacts with accompanying captions that reveal the everyday lives of the people and another titled "Gods and Demons" that is full of pictures of religious artifacts, with related captions.

So, I helped the students make a discovery similar to mine (see Figure 7.5). At the beginning of the lesson, I passed out the Sunday newspaper supplements, and after the students had an opportunity to browse for a moment, I asked them what they noticed about how the ads were organized. The student I called on

FIGURE 7.5. Advertisements and feature-packed informational text.

first nailed it immediately, responding, "Each page has only *one* kind of item on it, like jeans!" I then stated aloud, "So, if we had questions about what jeans are on sale, we would look at a particular page featuring jeans, right?" We continued by listing the groups of items the students noticed in the ads. Then I collected the advertisements and handed out the Kids Discover *Mesopotamia* (1999) texts. The students browsed for a few minutes, and then I asked the same question: "What do you notice about how these texts are organized?" There was a shift in the mood of the room as the students realized how similar these texts were to the advertising supplements.

Prior to looking at the advertisements, I had asked the students to fold blank sheets of 11″×17″ paper in a format similar to that described in Figure 7.2 (the sequence/time-order foldable). After they had discovered the organization of the Kids Discover text, I asked the students to get this foldable out to record their learning, and I shared my prepared model of the foldable with them. On the front of the first flap, I had used the first section heading in the book—"Day to Day"—to generate a question about what I would be learning: "What was day-to-day, or everyday, life like in Mesopotamia?" Inside I had written a summary paragraph with the author's central idea regarding the day-to-day life of the Mesopotamians and three supporting details I had gathered from the numerous observations on the two-page spread.

I put the model away because I wanted the group to generate their own notes and placed a copy of *Mesopotamia* under the document camera open to the two pages with the heading "Day to Day" (pp. 6–7). I thought aloud about the heading and the brief introduction and how I thought the author's central idea for these two pages was to reveal how ordinary citizens in Mesopotamia lived on a day-to-day basis. Predicting the author's purpose helped me set a purpose for reading—to find out how these ancient people lived every day. Then I modeled how I read or examined each of the features (illustrations, captions, boxed text) while keeping in mind my purpose for reading, and then I jotted down a few words about several of the artifacts and captions; the students, each with his or her own copy of the text, joined me, and then we engaged in the shared writing of notes. (It would be too much to try to take notes on every caption, illustration, or boxed text.)

Afterward, we returned to the foldables we had previously made and wrote the section's heading as a question on the front of the first flap. Before the students began writing inside the flap, I reminded them that to write a summary we needed to think about the author's central idea (which was also our purpose for reading) as well as the details in our notes that support the central idea. We engaged in the shared writing of the following summary (for the inside of the flap):

> Artifacts from ancient Mesopotamia reveal a lot about the everyday lives of the citizens. Some people lived in cities built with mud and brick and had all sorts of jobs, like being potters, carpenters, government officials, and priests. Other people lived outside the cities, raised animals, and farmed. There seemed to be a role for girls and a role for boys, and some families were like royalty, while other people were slaves.

Some students chose to copy this text inside the front flap of their folded notes, and others wrote their own summary. Then I asked the students to turn to the next two-page section in the text, titled "Demons and Gods." I posed the question "What do you need to do to understand this text?" With the advertisements and the demonstration in mind, they knew what to do. As the individual students finished reading, taking notes, and writing summaries, I asked each one to pick two more sections of the text (one for each flap on the folded note) to read, determine what was important, and then summarize. By the end of the lesson, many of the students had successfully tackled the text and were able to share aloud what they had learned.

■ What's Next?

If a student can determine what is important, then he or she can more easily compare and contrast different texts on the same subject. This is essential if the student wants to engage in research. Chapter 8 describes one way to help students read closely for specific information in multiple texts, take notes from multiple sources, and then use these notes to write a short research report.

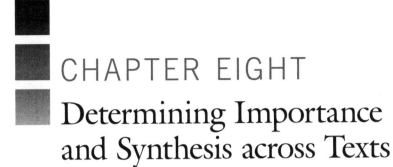

CHAPTER EIGHT
Determining Importance
and Synthesis across Texts

When I was visiting a fifth-grade classroom one day, I remember talking to two students who excitedly described to me their research report on hedgehogs. They delighted in saying that they had just finished reading several books about hedgehogs. When I asked them to tell me about the central ideas they were going to include in their report, however, their animated faces immediately fell blank. They had no idea! I immediately realized that they had been reading broadly *but without a specific purpose*—that is, there was just too much information for these students to manage.

What should one do? Nowadays, we rely on numerous resources to gather information on the subjects we find most important. The chances are that when we feel passionate enough to research a topic, we have specific questions in mind, questions that we have generated for ourselves, and, as proficient readers, we know when to skim and when to read closely. We have to teach our students how to do this as well, and yet this can be a very difficult process—not only for the learning but also for the teaching.

■ Consider Your Students' Strengths and Needs

What have your observations or formative assessments revealed about your students that leads you to believe they may need help in reading closely for information across texts and then summarizing and synthesizing what they have learned?

- When students confer with you about their research:
  - Do they struggle to generate their own questions to guide the research?
  - Do they talk about everything they have read about the subject?
  - Do they seem overwhelmed by all of the material they have encountered on the subject?
  - Do they articulate useful details they have uncovered in the text related to their research questions?
- When students write about what they have read in several texts:
  - Do they have a clear focus for their writing?
  - Do they accurately quote from the various texts on a subject?
  - Are they able to synthesize the information from the various sources and then restate it in their own words?

When our students research a subject, they need to be able to generate their own questions and consider what they already know about the right answers to these questions. Next, they need to be able to locate multiple texts (both online and offline) that provide information relevant to answering these questions. Once they locate the right texts, they need to understand that the information available can be overwhelming, and therefore they must skim the sources for relevant information and then slow down when needed to read closely. When reading closely, they need to determine what is important in the various texts, paraphrase what they have learned in personalized notes, and then consult their notes carefully when summarizing and synthesizing the information they have gathered.

■ Where to Start? Teaching Students How to Use I-Charts

The three lessons described in this chapter focus chiefly on:

1. Generating questions for a mini-research report.
2. Skimming and determining what is important in two teacher-selected texts and one student-selected text when undertaking to locate answers to the research questions.
3. Synthesizing the relevant information in notes taken from these sources in order to write a creditable report.

These lessons may be conducted over several work periods, depending on the specific needs of your students. For these lessons, students research answers to questions the whole class has generated on the same topic. Later as appropriate students can engage in the same process with independently selected topics during a unit of study. The primary instructional tool employed in these lessons is an inquiry chart (Hoffman, 1992), or I-chart. This graphic tool may be used to help organize a student's notes (see Figure 8.1); it can also serve as a map for the process students need to go through as they research the particular topic or issue. It can be used with a five-paragraph report or can be modified to support more in-depth reports. My recommendation is to work with students on composing well-written, tightly focused short reports before moving onto more extensive research and writing tasks.

In the first row of the chart, the student writes the key questions to be answered across the top row (additional columns may readily be added). In the second row, the student summarizes his or her prior knowledge regarding the answers to each question. In the next three rows (additional rows can be added for additional resources), the student writes the name of the resource in the first column and then the answers provided by each resource for each question. The final row summarizes the information gathered from all the resources for each question. The summaries often become the central ideas imported in the research

Student's name	Question #1	Question #2	Question #3
What I already know about the topic			
Resource #1			
Resource #2			
Resource #3			
Summary			

FIGURE 8.1. Minimized blank I-chart.

report. I suggest using large sheets of paper for I-charts so there is plenty of room for students to write.

In my experience, with most students it does not pay to simply hand them the chart, explain how to use it, and then leave them to work independently. There are just too many steps for most students to manage without close teacher guidance or scaffolding, including the following:

1. Generating possible research questions to consider.
2. Choosing three to four key questions to investigate more closely.
3. Writing about one's prior knowledge.
4. Locating reliable and relevant texts.
5. Skimming sources for the most relevant information in texts and then reading more closely.
6. Paraphrasing, in written notes, information from each text that helps answer key questions.
7. Continuing to skim and read closely and take notes while consulting resources.
8. Comparing, contrasting, and then summarizing the resulting information in writing.

Instruction needs to reveal how to break down this process—particularly during the first time that students are asked to systematically research a topic.

■ Lesson 1: Conceptualizing the Term *Research* and Generating Questions

Suggestions for Lesson Preparation and Text Study

- **Choose a core text.** Locate a text on a particular topic the whole group can use to generate and answer key questions. The choice of texts is very important. You want to start off with a text that is easily accessible to the students in terms of both instructional level and availability and one that suggests several interesting questions. In this way, they are more likely to start off successfully. For example, in the lesson with the fifth-grade students studing severe weather described later, I chose a magazine article on thunderstorms that had enough useful content to answer several interesting questions students might naturally pose. Otherwise, students might ask overly difficult or pointless questions and wander from text to text unsuccessfully looking for answers. By choosing a promising and accessible core text, they start with a foundation of answers that they can build on as they examine other texts.

- **Study the core text and plan for your think-aloud.** Read the core text, writing notes about the questions students might ask that would be answered in the text. Figure 8.2 illustrates the notes I prepared for my work with the fifth graders who were studying severe weather. I was planning for lessons on how to research and write a short report on severe thunderstorms. For a core text, I chose a *National Geographic Explorer* article titled "Storm Warning" (Brooks, 2010). As I read the article, I took notes about the questions students might generate. I noticed there was a lot of information that answered these particular questions:

  ○ What is a thunderstorm?

  ○ What tools or resources do meteorologists use to predict thunderstorms? What types of damage are caused by thunderstorms?

  ○ What are the *benefits* of thunderstorms?

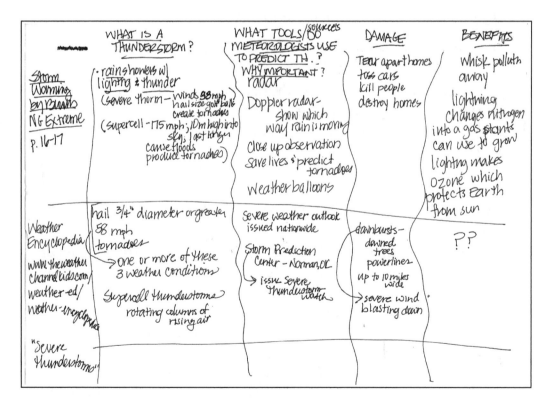

FIGURE 8.2. The notes I prepared for Lessons 1 and 2 with a group of fifth-grade students writing mini-reports on severe thunderstorms.

In my notes, you can see that I wrote the questions across the top of the paper and the answers from the core text on the first row. As a result of my preparation, I could also coach the students on the particular kinds of questions to ask. I would continue developing these notes when I located a second core text, as described in Lesson 2, below.

- **Create a visually accessible image** of the whole core text and an image of a blank I-chart for all the students to view as you take notes. As noted earlier, this might be most easily accomplished with a SMART Board, a document camera, an overhead projector, or an oversized piece of chart paper (for the I-chart).

- **Collect materials, including the following:** sufficient sets of the core text and of large sheets of paper (if possible 12″×18″ or larger—manila-colored paper or chart paper works best).

- **Plan to activate the students' background knowledge** on the topic of the core text.

Suggestions for Implementation of the Lessons

1. **Establish the purpose of the lesson.** These are the language objectives of the lesson that can be posted and explained in student-friendly language:
   - Ask the students to describe to their partner why someone might wish to engage in "research" on this topic or issue.
   - Ask them to talk to their partner about any questions they have concerning severe thunderstorms.
   - Generate questions with the group for our mini-research report.

2. **Activate background knowledge, and introduce the core text for the I-chart mini-research report.**
   - *Engage in activating prior knowledge on the topic.* For the fifth-grade class studying severe thunderstorms, I put together a five-slide PowerPoint presentation with fascinating photographs of thunderstorms. As I shared the pictures, I asked the students to talk to their partner about what they noticed in the pictures and what they already knew about the information on thunderstorms conveyed in the pictures.
   - *Pass out the core text, and ask the students to preview the text systematically* and to make predictions with their partner about the author's central ideas related to the topic.
   - *Ask the students to read the article independently or with a partner.* Remind

them to determine what is important as they read, and invite them to stop and share their thoughts with their partner at the end of each section in the text. This should be a familiar routine for the students by now, but, as always, be prepared to model and coach at the point of need. This is a good opportunity for you to read with small groups of students. It is not important for the students to be able to read this text closely and summarize at this point, because they will be reading it closely during the second lesson. They just need to begin to get a grasp of the ideas in the text.

3. **Explain the purpose of research and introduce I-charts.**

- *Introduce the purpose of the research with a real-life example.* From the beginning, students need to understand the purpose of the research and that the I-chart is a tool they can use to organize their thinking systematically. (Students may regard the I-chart as strictly a fill-in-the-blanks activity, and you need to correct this misimpression.) You might start this conversation by saying something like this:

> When we have questions about a particular topic, we engage in research to find answers. I know that when I have questions about an illness, I do a Google search on the Internet. I might be asking more than one question, like "What are the symptoms of this illness?" and "What does a person need to do to get better?" Usually I visit several Internet sites looking for information. I might also pull out a book I have on healthy living or a magazine that had an article on this illness as well. As I look through all of these sources, I don't read every single piece of information. I peruse or scan them for key words, perhaps in the headings, and then I skim the information; if I think a particular portion of the text is going to answer my question, I usually reread that section closely. This is what is meant by "research."

- *Brainstorm for questions with a shared think-aloud and shared writing.* Move next to the importance of asking certain key questions regarding the research topic (also the topic of the core text the students just read). You might say:

> There are a lot of questions we could ask when we research this topic. The first question I might ask is [share an example of a question from the notes you prepared], and I know I will find some answers in the text we just read.

Model writing the question you stated, and then continue by brainstorming for additional questions with the students and writing them down for all to view. See Figure 8.3 for the list of questions the fifth-grade students and I

What is a severe thunderstorm? ✗
Where do most thunderstorms occur?
How can we be safe in severe thunderstorms? ✗
How can a meteorologist predict a thunderstorm? ✗
How does a thunderstorm develop?
What kind of damage do these storms do?

FIGURE 8.3. An example of questions students generated with my support for a mini-research report on severe thunderstorms.

generated and that I wrote as we brainstormed for them to view. Remind the students to consider only questions that can be answered with the information from the text they have just read. As they generate suggested questions, ask the students to share aloud why the question is an important one to research. Coach them to notice whenever the question they suggest is actually redundant—that is, it solicits the same information as an earlier question—whenever it may not require much research (e.g., "yes" or "no" questions), or whenever questions should be grouped together because they are related in some way. These conversations help students realize they need to be mindful of the questions they ask when engaged in research.

• *Determine the key questions to research.* This is where you have to do some heavy guiding (especially the first time). You might say the following:

> When we are looking through multiple sources for information, it is helpful to narrow our list of questions to three and then look for answers to just *those* questions.

Help guide the students in choosing three questions from the larger brainstorming list; certain questions fit together more easily and make for a better report than others. As part of my instructional guidance, I also tell the students that I get to choose at least one of the questions (because I know they will be able to find answers in the core text, and I will be demonstrating how to do this during the following lesson). Circle or mark in some way the three questions. Students will need to copy these onto their I-charts. Figure 8.3 presents the list of questions I generated with the class studying severe thunderstorms. Notice the question "What is a severe thunderstorm?" and the arrow down to the question "How does a thunderstorm develop?" The students and I discussed how these two questions might be closely related. As the students and I decided on which three questions to select from the list for research, I drew a star next to each selection. Later, when the students drew their I-charts on large sheets of manila paper, they wrote these three questions across the top.

- *Create I-charts.* Direct the students to each fold a large sheet of paper (or they can just draw lines where the crease would be if they folded) so there are four columns and six rows on the chart. Guide them through writing the questions in the appropriate spaces in the top row. This might be a good opportunity for small groups of students to work together on one chart; everyone should commit to letting each person in the group write notes at some point during the process so that all are accountable for the group's efforts.

4. **Close the first lesson.** Finishing this chart will probably mark the end of the first lesson. If it is, be sure to close by asking the students to think aloud about what they did as readers and researchers during the lesson. It is important that they begin to recognize that certain preparatory steps are essential before reading texts closely to answer research questions. These steps include activating their own background knowledge (as they did when they read the core text), thinking through which questions are most important to answer, and creating a graphic organizer (the I-chart) to document their learning.

■ Lesson 2: Skimming and Then Reading Closely to Determine the Most Important Information in Multiple Texts

Suggestions for Lesson Preparation and Text Study

- **Prepare for a think-aloud with the core text.** Create a plan for how you will demonstrate skimming and then reading closely a particular section of core text (read by students during the first lesson) to determine the relevant important information that answers one of the key questions.

- **Locate a second core text.** Find a second text the students can use to answer key questions; each student will need a copy or at least ready access to this text. Be forewarned! There is no perfect text. Look for one the students can at least skim easily for important sections to read closely. For the mini-research report on severe thunderstorms, I found a short text on the Internet that served this purpose.

- **Determine other possible texts.** Either put together a text set that students can use to locate their third text (independently or with guidance) or compile a short list of websites that students can usefully visit to locate information. This requires doing your own skimming of texts to make sure that the students will find answers to at least one or more of the key questions. For the fifth-grade students, I chose five Internet sites, and then the classroom teacher and I checked out a class set of laptop computers and she set up access to these five sites.

Suggestions for Implementation of the Lesson

1. **Establish the purpose of the lesson.** These are the objectives of the lesson that can be posted and explained in student-friendly language:
   - Skim and read closely for information in three texts to answer the class's three research questions.
   - Write in your own words, or paraphrase, the important information that you find by reading closely.

2. **Activate the student's own background knowledge and review the core text for the I-chart mini-research project.**
   - *Getting started again.* Considering that this is the second lesson, review the steps taken in the preceding lesson to begin the research process. Use language like "activating background knowledge," "reading a text on the topic of the research," and "generating key questions" to describe the steps. Return everyone's I-charts, and review the questions the class as a whole chose to research.
   - *Ask the students to write* about what they already know regarding the answers to the three questions in the second row and then share with a partner.

3. **Explain the purposes of first skimming and then reading closely.**
   - *Activate the students' prior knowledge about determining what is important.* If you have previously engaged your students in lessons similar to those described in Chapter 7, they should be familiar with how to read closely to determine what is important. At this point, ask them to turn to a partner and remind each other what determining importance while reading "looks like." Language you should observe may include: "searching for key words and phrases to support the main idea," "looking for evidence in the text and

features to support what I think the author is trying to say," "paraphrasing or using my own words when I write notes about information in the text."

- *Project one page of the core text, and model skimming.* You might say the following:

> So, if I were to look back at this article for answers to my first question, would I reread the whole article? [Pause.] *No. What could I do?* [Pause.] *Maybe I should read section headings and think about whether I'll find answers in particular sections of the article? Let's look.*

Read aloud a section heading, and think aloud about why you think this section would or would not include information that would help you answer one of the research questions. Continue thinking aloud and engaging the students in a shared think-aloud until you reach a heading the group determines may have important information for answering one of the questions.

In the article on severe thunderstorms (Brooks, 2010), the fifth-grade students and I decided information under the heading "Birth of a Thunderstorm" might include answers to our question "What is a thunderstorm?" When we saw the subsequent section heading "Storm Chasers," however, we decided to read just the first sentence of each paragraph in that section because we were a little unsure whether the section's information would be relevant. The first sentence in the first paragraph was "We also use radar" (p. 15), and the first sentence of the third paragraph was "We also learn a lot about storms by getting next to, or even under, them" (p. 15). After reading each first sentence, we decided to read this section because it was about the tools and methods meteorologists use, and this would be useful information for answering our question "How can a meteorologist predict a severe thunderstorm?" We also took time to look at the features for important information. We soon realized we could use information in an illustration showing a person's hands holding "softball-size" hail (p. 15) to answer the first question.

When you and your students do locate a section of text that might be helpful, despite previous instruction on determining what is important, it is still a good idea to model how you would begin reading the text and to think aloud about what is important information. This think-aloud or demonstration would be similar to those modeled in Chapter 7. As before, mark your thinking on the projected text, underlining any key words.

- *Model writing notes on the I-chart.* Next, you want the students to transfer the words or phrases they thought were important to their correct locations on the I-chart. Think aloud about how you would write the key words and phrases from the text in notes to yourself on the enlarged I-chart that all students can view. Write a list of bulleted phrases. (I suggest modeling writing phrases for notes and not sentences because later you want your students to avoid copying their "sentences" directly from their notes straight into their report.)

4. **Engage the students in guided practice, with the teacher acting as the coach.**

   - *Skim together.* Begin to gradually release the students to work independently or in pairs. You may want to go back to thinking aloud about the different headings and determining, as a group, the next section that might be relevant before the students begin to work more independently.

   - *Coach for reading closely and taking notes.* Ask the students to determine what is important in the chosen section by reading independently or with a partner and then taking notes. When they are done, regroup and, as the students share, mark on the projected text the key words and phrases they chose. Discuss how they decided to take notes, and ask them to share their notes in small groups. Depending on the needs of your group, you may want to divide this process into separate steps. First, they read and determine what is important. Then, they regroup and discuss the key ideas. Then they take notes. And then finally they regroup and discuss their notes.

5. **Encourage independent or partner practice, and continue to coach or scaffold the students' learning.**

   - *Ask the students to "try it out on their own."* State explicitly the steps the students need to try out—continuing to skim for text that might provide answers to one of the three questions and then reading closely and taking notes.

   - *Move the students into a second core text.* As individuals or small groups finish locating answers in the first core text, give them the second core text to skim, then read closely. I find it helpful to ask the students to state explicitly what they plan to do with the text, and then I even observe as they start. (Warn the students that they may not find an answer to every question in each text they examine.)

   - *Provide access to a third text.* Whenever the students are ready, provide access to the text set or Internet links you have prepared in advance.

- *Confer continuously.* The conference scenarios and coaching suggestions in Chapter 7 (Table 7.1) should still be helpful. Other prompts to consider for this lesson include:

  > Tell me about what you are doing.
  >
  > What did you do when you found information that answered one of the questions?
  >
  > What do you need to do next? Why?

6. **Close the lesson with a conversation by synthesizing the knowledge that was developed and by reflecting on the strategic reading that was accomplished.**
   - *Regroup.* Ask the students to share in pairs or groups of three what they have learned about the topic or subject of the research. You may need to model how to share what they *learned*—versus simply *rereading their notes* aloud to their group. This will be especially important when the students have to write summaries of their notes. Nurture accountability by sitting with and listening to each group of students share.
   - *Close by restating the goals of the lesson* and summarizing how the group met those goals.

7. **Assess and plan your next lesson.**
   - The stages of development table in Chapter 7 (Table 7.2) might be helpful to consider at this point. Look through the students' I-charts, and assess whether they are listing the text's most important words and phrases. Determine whether you need to model again how to skim and read closely for particular answers or whether you need to model taking notes again.
   - If the students have completed their notes on the I-chart, you need to plan for how they will combine their notes into a coherent paragraph or two for each research question.

■ Lesson 3: Looking through the Notes to Summarize and Synthesize

This lesson teaches students how to synthesize the information they have located from more than one text. When students take notes and then write from those notes, they tend to start at the top of the notes and proceed to write a sentence for each bulleted item. Instead of following this approach, what they need to do is to read through all of the notes first and figure out which points or observations go together. Then they should combine these points or observations into a sentence or two. When the fifth-grade students finished taking notes on their I-charts, I planned a mini-lesson where I would think aloud about how to do just that. I chose one student's I-chart (Isabella's) to use during the mini-lesson (see Figure 8.4), and then I created a visually accessible image of Isabella's notes for one question, "What is a severe thunderstorm?"

In this case, the classroom had a SMART Board. I scanned Isabella's notes under the question "What is a severe thunderstorm?" and dropped them into the Notebook software. Then I projected her notes in front of the class with the SMART Board. For the purposes of this book, I retyped her notes in Figure 8.5. I made clear to the students that our goal for the day was to use our notes to write

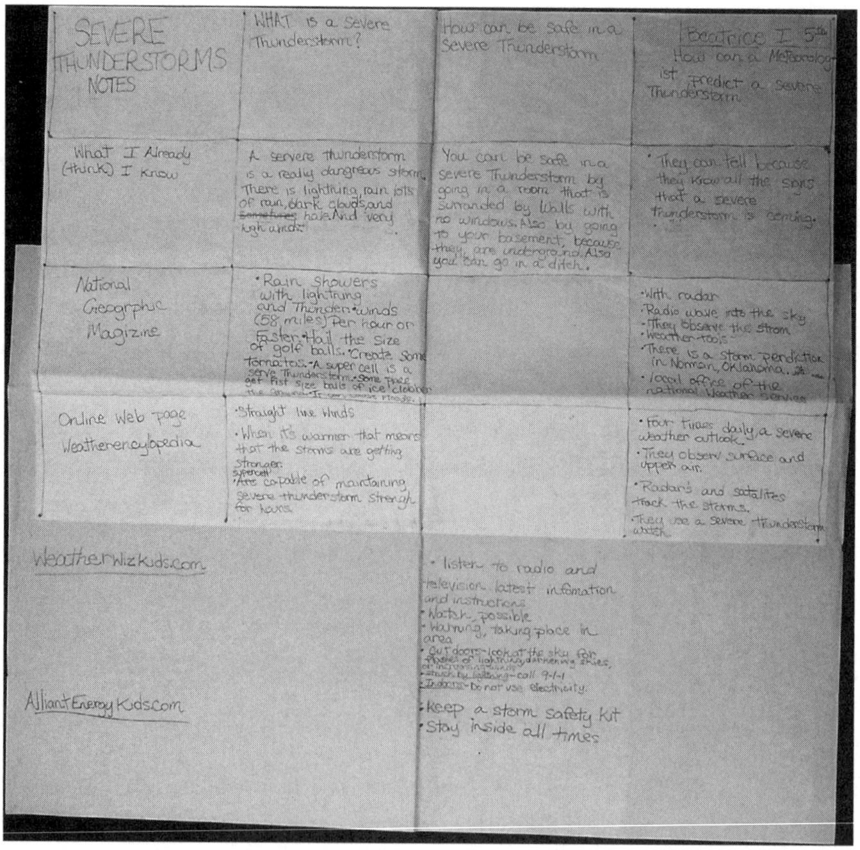

FIGURE 8.4. Isabella's I-chart.

SEVERE THUNDERSTORMS NOTES	What is a severe thunderstorm?
What I already know?	A severe thunderstorm is a really dangerous storm. There is lightning, lots of rain, dark clouds, and hail. And very high winds.
National Geographic article "Storm Warning" (Brooks, 2007)	• Rain showers with lightning and thunder • Winds (58 miles per hour) or faster • Hail the size of golf balls • Create some tornados • A super cell is a severe thunderstorm • Some places get fist sizeballs of ice clobber ground • It can cause floods
Internet site Weather Encyclopedia	• Straight line winds • When it's warmer that means the storms are getting stronger • Supercells are capable of maintaining severe thunderstorm strength for hours

FIGURE 8.5. Isabella's notes for the question "What is a severe thunderstorm?"

paragraphs that answered the research questions. I projected Isabella's notes and read them aloud to the students. Then I said the following:

> I could just write a sentence for each bulleted note and be done. [I pointed to the first bullet on the notes from the article and started listing my sentences in a monotone voice.] There are rain showers with lightning and thunder. Winds are 58 miles per hour or faster. Hail is the size of golf balls. Some create tornadoes. [I paused.] This does not sound very good, huh? I am all over the place. I don't have a clear direction. What can I do instead?

I entertained conversation with the students that moved us toward agreeing to group the notes into categories. We engaged in a shared writing (on the dry erase board next to the SMART Board) of the following paragraph:

> A severe thunderstorm can be a dangerous thunderstorm. A severe thunderstorm has rain showers, lightning, straight-line winds, and thunder. It can produce hail the size of a golf ball at ¾ of an inch. It has strong winds that can reach the speed of 58 miles per hour or more, and it can even create tornadoes. If the weather gets warmer, that means that the storm is likely getting stronger, and some thunderstorms, like a super cell, can stay strong for hours.

Notice how the paragraph we wrote incorporated notes from all three sections of the student's notes. Most of the sentences combine ideas from more than one point in the notes. There's also an additional fact that was not in Isabella's notes—"hail can be ¾ of an inch." When I called on a student to create a sentence aloud for our paragraph, he added this fact. We discussed that this fact was not in the notes but had been in our reading and was relevant. This was a good example of how a student may remember details that are not in the notes but still can incorporate those details into the summary writing when appropriate. Finally, we did not use every single note that Isabella wrote. We had a conversation about how we needed to think carefully about how we organized our paragraph and what we wanted to say. This meant that we did not have to include everything we had written in our notes.

For the next few lessons, the students typed essays from their notes. The classroom teacher followed up with mini-lessons on writing introductory and concluding paragraphs. In similar lessons with a group of fourth graders, I shared examples of the opening paragraphs of several magazine articles—lead paragraphs packed with vivid action words, sonorously repetitive ones, and dramatically descriptive ones (all calculated to grab the readers' attention!). In the end, the students had engaged in successful research and writing with a lot of instructional scaffolding. The trick is to help them engage in this process again and again and to nurture the students' agency and ultimate independence from such scaffolding.

Closing Thoughts

I would like to close by restating a few important points. Perhaps these points are the frame for the picture of instruction described in this book.

- *Teaching for close reading is essential if we want to create pathways to critical thinking and complex problem solving.* Students must be able to determine what is important at the sentence, paragraph, and section levels of a text in order to synthesize the key ideas in the text. Understanding the author's central ideas and how he or she has combined the supporting facts in a way that was calculated to convey those ideas best can empower students to critique those ideas, compare them to those of other authors, and take an informed stance.

- *Teaching for close reading is most successful when the lessons are naturally integrated into content-area learning.* Students understand texts better whenever they are able to apply their prior topical and vocabulary knowledge as well as the other skills involved in close reading to the task or assignment at hand. Close reading requires sustained energy on the part of the student. It plays a more distinctive role in larger, more meaningful projects or learning experiences, thereby further motivating students to engage in this activity.

- *An assessment-driven, structured approach to teaching provides the scaffolding and rigor students need to move forward in their learning.* Observing students during instruction and assessing their completed work both serve as guides for how best to plan and implement instruction at the point of need. In addition, studying the informational texts we are teaching and preparing carefully in advance both aids us in clearly articulating orally and in writing for our students during lessons. This creates a window for our students to observe and learn from proficient reading seen in action.

• *Building your students' comprehensive set of skills over time serves to sustain their progress in close reading.* Instruction with informational texts needs to be coherent and well organized, with each lesson building on the one before it. This continuous lesson plan is based on our assessment of students' use of strategies that are essential to close reading and our understanding of how we can move them forward. Every lesson, though, must engage our students in synthesis—the ultimate goal of all strategic reading.

The approaches to assessment and instruction that are advocated in this book require that teachers be totally focused on the learners. In my own professional experience with close reading, I have found the rewards of this kind of teaching to be well worth the effort expended. At the end of their 3-day cycle of lessons, the seventh-grade students who read the texts on global warming (as described in Chapter 4) wrote notes about their experiences with close reading. As I read through these notes, what popped out at me was the students' awareness of the value of close reading. Here are some of their comments:

> I think what we learned [about close reading] is helpful because I had never thought about it this way. This way with the sticky notes really helped me understand what we were reading better.

> What I did was I took small steps and I took notes and that helped me understand what this passage was about.

> When we took step by step helped me because I didn't read it all in a big lump.

> What I learned is important because if I had not learned this I would just read and not understand anything.

While I realize I was the guest teacher during these lessons (and thus on a "honeymoon" with the students to some extent), their comments *did* seem to reveal a genuine sense of intrigue at the difference close reading made for them. Over longer periods of close reading instruction, students begin to appreciate the importance of reading in new ways. They develop a closer affinity with the *act* of reading and are more eager to encounter the vast informational content that texts have to offer. They gradually view themselves as more capable readers and take on reading new texts with a greater sense of agency—a sense of "I can do this" or "I have lots of skills to tackle understanding this text well." They are more and more able to imagine a future in which they will be making decisions that will affect their (and our) world!

You can help sustain this conversation we have been having about teaching with informational texts by joining the professional learning community at my website (*www.Sunday-Cummins.com*). I look forward to hearing your thoughts and concerns and sharing in your celebrations.

APPENDIX
Study Guide

This study guide has been created to support and enhance your understanding of the instruction presented in this book. While as individuals each of you may find this helpful, the suggestions I make are primarily geared to professional learning communities (PLCs) of any kind, including grade-level and cross-grade-level teams with specialists, schoolwide teams, district-based teams, and groups of graduate students. Recommendations for instructional exercises and prompts for conversations are included for each chapter and can be followed in a sequence, or one may skip forward to particular chapters. The chief objective of this guide is simply to nurture conversations helpful to members' everyday practice. As part of this endeavor, each section of the guide suggests bringing your own teaching artifacts, instructional materials, and student work samples to the PLC meetings.

■ Chapter 1. What Does "Close Reading" Mean?

1. After reading this chapter, individually or with the members of your PLC, locate several informational texts that are available in your instructional setting. Engage in a close reading of selected sections of the texts. As you read, consider the following questions:

   • What skills are required for a reader to understand this text in depth?
   • How do the features and the main text collaborate in supporting each other?

- What are the author's central ideas? What evidence is provided to support those ideas?
- What obstacles might interfere with a student's understanding this text well?

2. As members of the PLC, dialogue with one another about various text types and determine which texts are better suited for close reading.

3. As a group or individually, set goals for teaching or observing close reading with students. Consider the following questions:

   - How can teaching close reading be better integrated into content-area units of study?
   - What should integrating literacy and content-area instruction "look like" when teaching close reading?
   - How can teams of teachers plan instruction that supports close reading throughout the day?

   Visit my website (*www.Sunday-Cummins.com*) for examples of sets of texts that have been grouped thematically for content-area units of study in science and social studies. These text sets include texts for reading aloud, excerpts of texts intended for close reading, and texts that can be made part of the classroom library (i.e., for general reading). Consider examining these text sets as a way of moving into conversations about how best to integrate literacy instruction with content-area instruction.

4. For additional reading on integrating literacy instruction with content-area instruction, consider reading and then discussing chapters from the following book:

   - McKee, J., & Ogle, D. (2005). *Integrating instruction: Literacy and science.* New York: Guilford Press.

5. If building students' vocabulary and background knowledge needs to be explored as part of your PLC's inquiry into close reading, these are suggested professional texts for further reading:

   - Blachowicz, C.L.Z., & Fisher, P. (2009). *Teaching vocabulary in all classrooms* (4th ed.). New York: Allyn & Bacon.
   - Buehl, D. (2011). *Developing readers in the academic disciplines.* Newark, DE: International Reading Association.
   - Fisher, D., & Frey, N. (2009). *Background knowledge: The missing piece of the comprehension puzzle.* Portsmouth, NH: Heinemann.

■ Chapter 2. An Assessment-Driven, Structured Approach to Teaching

1. Read and discuss Chapter 2 with members of your PLC. As you read this chapter, reflect on how the instruction described compares with your own. Consider the following questions:

   • What have you observed your students doing as close readers?
   • How do you scaffold instruction in close reading when teaching with informational texts?
   • What do you do to prepare in advance for this instruction?
   • What, if anything, is missing in your instructional practices?

2. Meeting as a PLC, have a conversation about the instructional practices described in this chapter. Additional questions to consider include:

   • What types of support do you and your colleagues need to enhance your teaching with informational texts that you are not already receiving?
   • How can you best support one another?

3. Locate a video of an educator teaching how to understand informational text or develop a video of one member of the PLC teaching. As you view the videos with the other members of your PLC, take three-column notes as follows:

What is the teacher saying? What actions does the teacher take?	How does the teacher's language and actions serve to support the students?	How does this resonate with my practice? What are questions that I have?
Example of notes about language: The teacher says, "When I tackle a text like this, I start by previewing the whole text. Let me show you how I do this."	*Example of notes about language:* The teacher is putting herself or himself out there as a reader—showing the students what she does as a reader. She is also being explicit about what she does.	*Examples of notes:* I usually am explicit about what the student should be doing as a reader, but I am telling the student what a reader does. I am not saying what *I* do as a reader. I wonder if that makes a difference.
Example of notes about actions: The teacher places the transparency of the excerpt from the text on an overhead projector. As she talks, she draws arrows next to the features she has previewed.	*Example of notes about actions:* Students can actually see how she previews the text when she marks on the text.	I don't always have an image of the text posted in some way for all the students to see. When I do, I point to the text, but I do not mark on the text as a visual for what a reader needs to do. I need to think about doing that.

After the video clip, debrief yourselves as a group. Consider the following questions:

- What connections could be drawn between the group members' observations?
- What themes were apparent in the purposes of the scaffolding described?
- What instructional changes might you need to consider implementing?

■ Chapter 3. Introducing Synthesis with Interactive Read-Alouds

1. Individually or as members of the PLC, locate and read several high quality informational books available in your school or at the public library. Consider these questions:

   - What makes these texts appealing?
   - How might they fit into the content-area units you are already teaching?
   - What are the authors' central ideas? What evidence in each text supports these ideas?
   - What would you say in thinking aloud about your synthesis of each text?

2. Individually or with support, plan for and implement an interactive read-aloud, introducing the students to synthesis by means of the framed picture analogy. If you have already been reading aloud information texts to your students and talking about synthesis, use your experience to consider the specific ideas elaborated in this chapter. What does the content of this chapter offer that you might want to consider introducing into your own practice? Plan and implement a lesson based on your reflection on your particular instructional practices.

3. Bring the text from the lesson and any related teaching artifacts or student writing samples to your PLC meeting. Consider engaging in the following experiences:

   - Have a conversation about the lessons that individual members have implemented. What went well? Which aspects of your own instructional practices might benefit from modifications?
   - Take time to look through your own students' work using the four stages of development schema described in the chapter (Table 3.2) to assess your students' responses. What do you notice? What might a future lesson—small-group or whole-class—look like, based on your observations?
   - Consider making a commitment to return to the PLC later with additional teaching artifacts and student responses from a subsequent lesson. The protocol in the box Looking at Your Students' Work can be used to guide these discussions.

Looking at Your Students' Work

Prior to this meeting, each member will have selected one student's work to share with the group. One person in the group agrees to keep track of the time and to help the group stay focused on following the time schedule and agenda. If time permits, members will *take turns* sharing their students' work during the same meeting. The description below includes the recommended steps, suggested questions to help direct what is shared and discussed, and the recommended time allowance for each step. Groups should feel free to modify this protocol to best meet their individual needs.

PROTOCOL

1. **Teacher presents.** What has the teacher already noticed about this student? What was the assignment? What did the teacher notice in the student's written work? (2 minutes)
2. **Group analyzes.** What is the student doing well? What does the student need to work on? (5 minutes)
3. **Group brainstorms.** What instruction might help this student? (5 minutes)
4. **Teacher plans.** When and how will this happen in the classroom? (2 minutes)
5. **Group draws conclusions.** How might a similar approach work for student(s) in other members' classrooms? (5 minutes)

Based on the work of Blythe, Allen, and Powell (2008).

4. For additional reading and dialogue, locate and study the following articles:

   - Cummins, S., & Stallmeyer-Gerard, C. (2011). Teaching for synthesis of informational texts with read-alouds. *The Reading Teacher, 64*(6), 394–405.
   - Cummins, S. (2011). Using *Choice Words* in nonfiction reading conferences. *Talking Points, 22*(2), 9–14.

5. For additional samples of students' written responses to texts read aloud, visit *www. Sunday-Cummins.com*.

■ Chapter 4. Understanding the Features of a Text

1. As a PLC, read and discuss Chapter 4. Extend this discussion by examining features in texts that you locate in your school or local public library. Consider the following questions:

   - How should the reader deal with the typical two-page spread? Reading top to bottom? Left to right? Clockwise?
   - How do the features support the main text?

- How does the information provided in the features individually and the running text work to support and reinforce one another?
- How do the text's accompanying features work to support one another?

2. Individually or with colleagues' support, plan a lesson or cycle of lessons based on the ideas in Chapter 4. Implement the lessons, and collect the resulting instructional artifacts and the students' responses.

3. With another teacher or individually, look through the students' work completed during the lesson(s) and choose three to five examples of student work that range from the attempting level to the meeting or exceeding (expectations) level. Plan to share these at a PLC meeting.

4. Acting collectively as a PLC, have a conversation about the lesson(s) implemented. Consider these questions:

- How did the individual members of the PLC make a visually accessible image for the students to see during the think-aloud?
- What was the flow of each member's think-aloud like? Did the students want to join in a shared think-aloud? How did the members maintain an ongoing dialogue with their students?

5. Acting collectively as a PLC, look closely at your students' work samples. Using the stages of development described in Chapter 4 (Table 4.3), ask yourself:

- What are the students revealing about their understanding of features? What do their responses include about the author's central ideas?
- How might you move individual students forward in their effective use of features?
- Consider making a commitment to return later to the PLC with instructional artifacts and students' responses from an additional lesson. What evidence could each member of the PLC bring to show that his or her students are making progress?

■ Chapter 5. Strategic Previewing of a Text to Set a Purpose

1. Individually or with your PLC, practice or rehearse using the THIEVES approach to previewing and predicting with a text that your students will likely be reading in the near future. After previewing the text systematically, read the text. Discuss the following questions:

- What did you notice about yourself as a reader after you previewed the text strategically?
- How might this approach be helpful to your students?

2. Plan and implement a lesson with THIEVES. If you have already taught your students a previewing strategy, consider how you might review this strategy for more effective use by the students.

3. Use the stages of development learning continuum described in Chapter 5 (Table 5.3) to assess your students' previewing and predicting. What kind of instruction do they need to move them forward?

4. Individually, plan and implement a follow-up lesson based on your assessment of your students' learning from the first lesson.

5. Acting collectively as a PLC, have members bring artifacts from both lessons. Discuss the following:

- What did you notice during the first lesson? What about afterwards, when you looked at students' responses?
- How did you address these observations during the next lesson?
- What did you notice after the second lesson when you analyzed your students' work?

■ Chapter 6. Self-Monitoring While Reading Informational Texts

1. Read and discuss Chapter 6 with your PLC colleagues. Consider these questions during your dialogue:

- What have you noticed during interactions with your students that reveals whether they are self-monitoring while reading informational texts?
- What have you already done to teach them how to self-monitor? What have you noticed as a result?
- Based on the content of this chapter, what might be missing from your assessment of students' self-monitoring? From your own instruction?

2. If your students need to work on self-monitoring, plan and implement a lesson on how to use the coding method. Plan specifically to confer with your students during the guided practice sessions as well as during independent study. Use Table 6.1, which describes several common conferring scenarios, as a reference for what you

might notice and say during conferences with your students. As you meet with them individually, take anecdotal notes about your conversations with them.

- What did they say?
- What did you say to prompt their thinking?
- How did this exchange move the student forward (or not)?

3. Bring your anecdotal notes to your PLC meeting. Dialogue with your peers about what you observed and said during the conferences.

- What seemed to be helpful?
- What was still puzzling?
- What do you need to continue to do when conferring with students?
- What do you need to do more of when conferring with students? Less of?

■ Chapter 7. Determining Importance in a Text

1. Consider modifying and implementing the study guide suggestions for Chapter 4, suggestions 2–5, on page 182 as they relate to Chapter 7.

2. Also, consider videotaping yourself teaching a mini-lesson on determining what is important on the basis of the ideas in Chapter 7. Then, after watching the video by yourself or with a partner, ask yourself:

- What do you observe yourself doing that makes clear to students what a proficient reader does to determine what is important?

3. Share a 3- to 5-minute video clip of your instructional techniques with your PLC. Agree as a group in advance what you will be looking for in each member's clip, whether it's how one interacts with the visually accessible images of the text or what one says exactly during the think-aloud portion of the mini-lesson. Engage with members in a nonevaluative dialogue about each video clip, which might include members reading from their notes, asking one another questions, or sharing anecdotes from their own practice. The objective would solely be to affirm and broaden members' collective practice experience. The protocol dcescribed earlier can be modified for these conversations.

▨ Chapter 8. Determining Importance and Synthesis across Texts

1. Basing your work on the content in Chapter 8, plan and implement lessons that move students through reading and writing a mini-research report that involves multiple texts as sources.

2. Meet as a PLC several times during this series of lessons. Consider bringing any relevant instructional artifacts and student work samples to the group's meetings to reference during the discussions. The likely topics for discussion include:

   • How instruction looks that most helps students generate questions for research.
   • How teachers can best create visually accessible images of text for think-alouds about skimming and determining where to read closely.
   • What students reveal in their I-charts about their skills in determining what is important (you should review Chapter 7, on determining what is important, before undertaking this topic).
   • How students should combine notes from multiple sources in developing their summaries and how instruction can best be shaped to support students in this task.

3. Make a commitment to return to the PLC in the future with instructional artifacts and students' work from any additional lessons. Each member should bring whatever evidence best shows that his or her students are continuing to make progress in close reading and synthesizing the most relevant information.

References

ACT, Inc. (2006). *Reading between the lines: What the ACT reveals about college readiness in reading.* Iowa City, IA: Author.

Afflerbach, P., Pearson, P. D., & Paris, S. G. (2008). Clarifying differences between reading skills and reading strategies. *The Reading Teacher, 61*(5), 364–373.

Allington, R. (2009). *What really matters in response to intervention: Research-based designs.* New York: Allyn & Bacon.

Armbruster, B. B., McCarthey, S. J., & Cummins, S. (2005). Writing to learn in elementary classrooms. In R. Indrisano & J. R. Paratore (Eds.), *Learning to write, writing to learn: Theory and research into practice* (pp. 71–96). Newark, DE: International Reading Association.

Aronson, M. (2011). *Trapped: How the world rescued 33 miners from 2,000 feet below the Chilean desert.* New York: Atheneum Books.

Bellanca, J., & Brandt, R. (Eds.). (2010). *21st century skills: Rethinking how students learn.* Bloomington, IN: Solution Tree Press.

Bishop, N. (2008). *Frogs.* New York: Scholastic Nonfiction.

Bishop, N. (2010). *Lizards.* New York: Scholastic Nonfiction.

Blachowicz, C. L. Z., & Fisher, P. (2009). *Teaching vocabulary in all classrooms* (4th ed.). New York: Allyn & Bacon.

Blythe, T., Allen, D., & Powell, B. S. (2008). *Looking together at student work.* New York: Teachers College Press.

Brooks, H. (2010). Storm warning. *National Geographic Explorer! Extreme, 3*(6), 12–17.

Brummett, B. (2010). *Techniques for close reading.* Thousand Oaks, CA: Sage.

Buehl, D. (2011). *Developing readers in the academic disciplines.* Newark, DE: International Reading Association.

Burgan, M. (2008). *Illinois.* New York: Children's Press.

Cazden, C. B. (2001). *Classroom discourse: The language of teaching and learning.* Portsmouth, NH: Heinemann.

Clay, M. M. (1993). *Reading recovery: A guidebook for teachers.* Portsmouth, NH: Heinemann.

Collard, S. B., III. (2005). *The prairie builders: Reconstructing America's lost grasslands.* Boston: Houghton Mifflin.

Common Core State Standards Initiative. (2010). *Common Core State Standards for English language arts & literacy in history/social studies, science, and technical subjects.* Washington, DC: National Governors Association Center for Best Practices and the Council of Chief State School Officers.

Cummins, S. (2011). Using *Choice Words* in nonfiction reading conferences. *Talking Points, 22*(2), 9–14.

Cummins, S., & Stallmeyer-Gerard, C. (2011). Teaching for synthesis of informational texts with read-alouds. *The Reading Teacher, 64*(6), 394–405.

Deem, J. M. (2008). *Bodies from the ice: Melting glaciers and the recovery of the past.* Boston: Houghton Mifflin.

Echevarria, J., & Graves, A. (2007). *Sheltered content instruction: Teaching English language learners with diverse abilities* (4th ed.). New York: Pearson, Allyn & Bacon.

Echevarria, J., Vogt, M., & Short, D. J. (2004). *Making content comprehensible for English learners: The SIOP model.* New York: Pearson.

Englert, C. S., Mariage, T. V., & Dunsmore, K. (2006). Tenets of sociocultural theory in writing instruction research. In C. A. MacArthur, S. Graham, & J. Fitzgerald (Eds.), *Handbook of writing research* (pp. 208–221). New York: Guilford Press.

Finkelman, P. (2004). *The Constitution.* Washington, DC: National Geographic School Publishing.

Fisher, D., & Frey, N. (2008). *Better learning through structured teaching.* Alexandria, VA: ASCD.

Fisher, D., & Frey, N. (2009). *Background knowledge: The missing piece of the comprehension puzzle.* Portsmouth, NH: Heinemann.

Fisher, D., Frey, N., & Lapp, D. (2008). *In a reading state of mind: Brain research, teacher modeling, and comprehension instruction.* Newark, DE: International Reading Association.

Freeman, D., & Freeman, Y. (2007). *English language learners: The essential guide.* New York: Scholastic.

Fu, D. (2009). *Writing between languages: How English language learners make the transition to fluency, grades 4–12.* Portsmouth, NH: Heinemann.

Geiger, B. (2010). Thirsty planet. *National Geographic Explorer! Pathfinder, 10*(2), 18–23.

George, J. C. (2008). *The wolves are back.* New York: Dutton Children's Books.

Goodman, S. E. (2008). *See how they run: Campaign dreams, election schemes, and the race to the White House.* New York: Bloomsbury U.S.A. Children's Books.

Guiberson, B. Z. (2009). *Life in the boreal forest.* New York: Holt.

Headley, K. (2008). Improving reading comprehension through writing. In C. C. Block & S. R. Parris (Eds.), *Comprehension instruction: Research-based best practices* (2nd ed., pp. 214–225). New York: Guilford Press.

Hillocks, G. (2011). *Teaching argument writing: Grades 6–12.* Portsmouth, NH: Heinemann.

Hoffman, J. V. (1992). Critical reading/thinking across the curriculum: Using I-charts to support learning. *Language Arts, 69*(2), 121–127.

Hoyt, L. (2008). *Revisit, reflect, retell: Time-tested strategies for teaching reading comprehension.* Portsmouth, NH: Heinemann.

Jenkins, M. (2003). *Grandma elephant's in charge.* Cambridge, MA: Candlewick Press.

Johnson, R. L. (2002). *Global warming.* Washington, DC: National Geographic School Publishing.

Johnston, P. H. (2004). *Choice words: How our language affects children's learning.* Portland, ME: Stenhouse.

Kids Discover. (1999). *Mesopotamia.* New York: Author.

Manz, S. L. (2002). A strategy for previewing textbooks: Teaching readers to become THIEVES. *The Reading Teacher, 55*(5), 434.

Mattern, J. (2009). *Illinois: Past and present.* New York: Rosen Central.

McClafferty, C. K. (2011). *The many faces of George Washington: Remaking a presidential icon.* Minneapolis, MN: Carolrhoda Books.

McKee, J., & Ogle, D. (2005). *Integrating instruction literacy and science.* New York: Guilford Press.

Montgomery, S. (2010). *Kakapo rescue: Saving the world's strangest parrot.* New York: Houghton Mifflin Books for Children.

Patent, D. H. (1996). *Prairies.* New York: Holiday House.

Plimoth Plantation. (2003). *Mayflower 1620: A new look at a Pilgrim voyage.* Washington, DC: National Geographic.

Reid, R., & Lienemann, T. O. (2006). *Strategy instruction for students with learning disabilities.* New York: Guilford Press.

Ruane, M. E. (2010). KABOOM! *National Geographic Explorer! Pathfinder, 10*(2), 10–17.

Sandler, M. (2012). *Freaky-strange buildings.* New York: Bearport.

Sandler, M. W. (2009). *The Dust Bowl through the lens: How photography revealed and helped remedy a national disaster.* New York: Walker.

Santella, A. (2002). *All around Illinois: Regions and resources.* Minneapolis, MN: Heinemann Library.

Short, D. J. (2002). Language learning in sheltered social studies classes. *TESOL Journal, 11*(1), 18–24.

Simon, S. (1999). *Icebergs and glaciers.* New York: HarperCollins.

Simon, S. (2007). *Spiders.* New York: Collins.

Spielvogel, J. J. (2005). *Glencoe world history.* New York: McGraw-Hill.

Stephens, C. (2002). *The human machine.* Washington, DC: National Geographic School Publishing.

Swain, R. (2003). *How sweet it is and was: The history of candy.* New York: Holiday House.

Swanson, H. L., & Hoskyn, M. (2001). Instructing adolescents with learning disabilities: A component and composite analysis. *Learning Disabilities Research and Practice, 16*(2), 109–119.

Swanson, H. L., Kehler, P., & Jerman, O. (2010). Working memory, strategy knowledge, and strategy instruction in children with reading disabilities. *Journal of Learning Disabilities, 43*(1), 24–47.

Swanson, H. L., & Sachse-Lee, C. (2000). A meta-analysis of single-subject-design intervention research for students with LD. *Journal of Learning Disabilities, 33*(2), 114–136.

Taylor-Butler, C. (2009). *Sacred mountain: Everest.* New York: Lee & Low Books.

Toulmin, S. E. (2003). *The uses of argument.* Cambridge, UK: Cambridge University Press.

Turbill, J., & Bean, W. (2006). *Writing instruction K–6: Understanding process, purpose, audience.* Katonah, NY: Richard C. Owen.

Turner, P. S. (2011). *The frog scientist.* Boston: Sandpiper.

Vygotsky, L. S. (1978). *Mind in society: The development of higher psychological processes.* Cambridge, MA: Harvard University Press.

Wiggins, G., & McTighe, J. (2005). *Understanding by design.* Upper Saddle River, NJ: Pearson Education.

Winkler, P. (2004). *Animal adaptations.* Washington, DC: National Geographic School Publishing.

Zwiers, J. (2004). *Building reading comprehension habits in grades 6–12: A toolkit of classroom activities.* Newark, DE: International Reading Association.

Index

Page references in italic refer to tables and figures.